6

Brenda,

Hope you get
a blast
from this!

Peace, love & tie-dye,

Johnny Rockit

5/99

# KOLINAR

# The Rock'n'Roll State of Mind

## Johnny Rockit

# KOLINAR
The Rock'n'Roll State of Mind

ADVANCE COPY

Illustrations by Neal Berg, David Chrone, Ed Ott, and Holly Vesely. Cover artwork by Krista Dodson and Ed Ott.

With love to Catherine Benejet.

Muchas gracias to Clark Redwoods.

Special thanks to Ruce & Sharon Mallet, Amy Jane Mews, Helen Goblet, J&D Snowman, and The Family.

Also thanks to Richard Reed, Aladin Salt, Reba Rebel, and Todd Burke.

With heartfelt gratitude to my parents, Frank and Penny, and sister, Maggie.

Published by:     Bayshore Enterprises, Inc.
                  P.O. Box 937
                  Boca Raton, Florida 33429
                  1-(888) 565-4627

                  ISBN No. 1-892654-13-X

For

Rock'n'Roll

Party Animals

# FORWEIRD

Nothing you have ever done in your life
has adequately prepared you
for what you are about to experience.

The Rock'n'Roll State of Mind is finally here!
Yes! That's right! The one you've been waiting for!
It's here! This is it! We've arrived! HooooRaayyy!

Your journey to the exalted State of Kolinar
*begins with this book.*
Designed with you, the party animal, in mind,
each chapter is short,
to match your attention span,
and has no correlation with the other chapters,
to avoid taxing your memory.
There is no plot
(except the one to relieve you of your sanity).

The result?  An experience totally focused on
the **present**;  the **now**;
the ever-unfolding transplendent *moment* that is your
**own** personal doorway
to all-encompassing magnificence.

And, you can *have it all*, without giving up the fast cars,
hot guitars, and wild parties!

With KOLINAR-----The Rock'n'Roll State of Mind!

----THE EDITORS

# Preface

"With surprisingly few exceptions, major scientists believe we should investigate the possibility of terraformation, though many doubt that Mars could be renovated for a price this planet can afford. The investment will be large, but the return could be prodigious."

"...They propose that the United States, the Soviet Union, Europe and Japan attempt the most ambitious engineering project in human history: the 'terraformation' of Mars, the greening of the red planet. They want to transform Mars into a new home for humankind---and they believe they can do it in less than two centuries."

"...The human brain has a formidable record of accomplishment. But it may never have confronted a challenge as awesome as the terraformation of Mars. We will have to raise the entire planet's temperature by 100 degrees F, transmute its girdle of lethal gas into an atmosphere humans can breathe, erect a global shield against solar radiation, build heavy industries on Martian soil, construct farms and cities in biosphere bubbles, and transport thousands of people, plants and animals to Mars in a fleet of interplanetary arks. Even the most eager partisans are abashed by the size of the undertaking, but there is rough agreement on how it might be accomplished. The views of dozens of leading space scientists are reflected in this six-stage scenario."

--- LIFE Magazine, May, 1991

# The Rock'n'Roll State of Mind

## Starring

## The New Cosmic Sound

# i. INTRODUCTION

**by Johnny Rockit**

Hey, man. This is for you. Check it out.
Life, the Universe, and Ultimate Reality
have finally come down to our level.

We've got the heartbeat of the new America here,
all you people who go to rock concerts.

We've got some wings for you,
and a halo too.

Why just follow these instructions
to a new vibration
and you'll get radical illumination.

Like, wow, man. It's totally awesome!
You can amaze your friends!
Impress people at parties!
Be the envy of everyone!

And you can turn up your nose at all those other
milktoast high-brow cosmologies.

Because *now* you've *got*
the **one** that's **hot** —
KOLINAR!
Not that this is trendy or anything.

This is for all you low-life sleazebags who do nothing but water ski, surf, play rock'n'roll, party, and read TV Guide. You "know there's something more to life" (even though you don't *do* anything about it).

Now you can say you read a **book** this year! Wow! That oughtta impress the hell out of everybody.

Until they find out which one. Reading *this* trash isn't gonna give you status. If it does, your friends are scary. This is one notch above reading comic books.

The Party Book. Party on the pages. The book that was supposed to be a tutorial on the ultimate meaning of life, but turned out to be nothing but pages of gibberish.

But some of you may be saying, "That's okay. This is fine the way it is. It can go on like this for a long time." You people must be from the Too Close To The Speakers Club.

Actually, I won't tell you where the gibberish ends and the tutorial begins. But there will be a test at the end of the book.

And we won't just cover outer space. We'll cover oral sex, too, and anything else that's important. So check it out! KOLINAR!! It's ALIVE! Aaaaggghhh! Kill it before it multiplies!

And listen.

I'm not a senator.

I'm not an industrial conglomeration.

I'm not one of Them.

I'm a rocker.

A stratoblaster.

Johnny Rockit.

Alias Johnny DeGenerate, latent rock'n'roll animal.

Your host on this one way ticket to Zorbitron.

I don't have any big vested interest in The Way Things Are.

So, we're going to blow the covers off The Way Things Are. And show you the magical "Other World" that lies *beneath the surface* of The Way Things Are, or appear to be! Ooooooooohhh!

So come on! The party's just beginning!

Let's Gooooooooo!

# HOW TO DECIDE IF THIS BOOK IS FOR YOU

1.  Picture your life from the moment of puberty up until this very instant and see if there are any rock concerts in it.

☐ YES - I can picture them now.  Ahhh! Wonderful!
☐ **NO - I ain't neva bin to no rok concet.**

2.  If your answer is "Yes," and you managed to make it through High School, then YES, *Go Ahead* and take the book.  Go for it.  Take it!

3.  If your answer is "No," then this book is not for you and you can put it back now.

4.  If you don't know the answer, or you can't remember any further back than last week, take the book.
You need it, buddy.

5.  If you're past 18, but you haven't reached puberty, put this book back and get one on stamp collecting.

6.  If you're over 21, but you're still mentally **at** the instant of puberty, take the book and join the club.


OKAY!
HELLO, FELLOW ROCKERS!
LET'S PARRRDEEE!

# 1. ROCK CONCERT

Clark, Amy, Bruce, Karin, Brad, and Paula reached their
seats just in time.
The house lights dimmed.
The crowd cheered.
*This place is alive*, thought Clark.
*The atmosphere is electric*, Amy echoed.
The lights went out.
It was dark.
The cheering intensified.
All of a sudden, what looked like hundreds of candles
started appearing in the darkness.
Hundreds of flames burning in the night
at every level, high and low,
all around the huge cavernous pitch black hall.

*There's enough energy going around in here*
*to light a city*, Karin imagined.
*And there's only one thing more powerful*
*than the cheering.*
*The Music.*

Lightning struck the dark stage, and
in a flash of excitement the band came on, thundering.
*God, it's finally loud enough*, Clark told himself.
*After months of listening to my home stereo*
*at low volume so I don't blow away my neighbors—*
*it's finally loud enough.*

It's rock'n'roll unchained.
Set free. Played the way it's supposed to be.
Loud.
Not too loud.
Perfectly loud.
Loud enough to wrap you in its wings,
engulf you in eargasm,
and take you away.


Bruce looked around him and drank it in.
His 9 to 5 job was somewhere on another planet now.
All he heard was the cheering of the crowd.
A geyser of joy swelled up in his chest and he hollered:
 "Rock Concert!
 Other guys with long hair!
 A lotta sexy girls in tight pants!
 Ten Thousand People Playing Air Guitar!
 I'm Here!
 I'm Home!
 Yaaa Hoooo!"
Paula took out her binoculars and checked out the stars.
*They look terrific*, she thought.
*Better than on the album cover. True heroes.*
And she watched them, thinking:
*They're having a blast up there.*
*They're fresh. They're feisty. They're foxy.*
*They're incredibly good.*


And she pictured herself up there with them,
living their life, playing that music,
and drinking in the wild cheering of the crowd.

"This is a *GREAT* concert!" she raved, passing Brad the binoculars.

"The band is *BETTER* live than on the albums!" he howled.

As Brad looked through the glasses, Paula thought,

*The sound is perfectly balanced.*
*You can hear every instrument*
*and every voice*
*distinctly*
*in just the right proportion to each other.*
*No voice or instrument*
*is overpowering or inaudible.*
*It's all there, perfect, just the way it should be.*

Brad swung the glasses away from the stage and checked out the guys in the mixing booth. They had beards and were wearing headsets. They were concentrating on the band and moving levers on control panels hazed in a greenish glow.

*They are stars too*, Brad thought. *Would I trade my life for theirs? In a minute. ......Especially considering the* *BABES around the mixing booth. Drop-dead gorgeous plutonium blondes that'll melt steel. Mouth-watering tropical brunettes in outfits that'll take your breath away. I thank the Universe for rock'n'roll women — they're the finest in the world!*

Brad's reverie was interrupted by Amy, who was tapping on his arm for the glasses. He handed her the binoculars, and the band revved into a new number. The energy of the music surged through Brad and Amy's bodies like an invisible wave breaking over them in the night. The vocals were clean, the harmony was tight, the rhythm was crisp, and the guitar work was flawless. The whole crowd was on its feet, dancing to the music, clapping their hands, whistling, stomping, and playing air guitar!

*This is the finest thing 10,000 people can do together*, Amy realized.

A vibrant blue-green laser gridwork suddenly emanated from behind the band, and fanned out into space over the whole coliseum. Now the music exploded skyward in a spiraling harmonic crescendo synchronized with the lasers. Clark, Karin and Bruce all hollered in unison:
> "This is cosmic!
> This is too much!
> This is Ultimate Reality!"

Bruce carried on:
"If Men from Space landed
in the middle of the concert now,
people from a world much more advanced than ours,
you'd be proud to be a human
with this music and this crowd."

Karin hooted:
"Wanna know what Earth is like, Mr. Space Man?
Check out this concert.
Tape *this* and take it back to the Plieades, pardner.
This place is bitchin'!"

"Wanna scan this crowd for energy?" Clark jeered.
"Go ahead. . . . .
Ohhh, broke your sensors?  Too bad...."
"Check it out, buddy," Brad yelled.
"ROCK'N'ROLL THE PLACE!!!"

# 2.  HOW TO PRONOUNCE ZVORTYL *

As Amy walked out into the night air after the concert, there was a humming in her head.  She looked around the coliseum parking lot, and it seemed misty and surreal, as if underwater.  Her friends' voices and the other sounds outside seemed muffled, as if she were wearing earphones, and her mind was blank.  She felt like her feet were walking on pillows.  She was smiling for no apparent reason, and her eyes were slightly glazed.

Paula walked up to her.  "Congratulations," she said. "You are experiencing *The Zvortyl Effect*.  You have evolved to a lower form of life.  You are one of us, now."

Amy smiled a glazed smile.  "Come on," Paula said, and they walked across the parking lot to Paula's van.  Clark, Bruce, Karin and Brad arrived moments later, and everyone piled into the van and took off for Zen-Sun's ice cream parlor.  Paula's favorite radio station was doing instant replays of hits from the concert, and everybody in the van began making barnyard animal noises over the music (especially the *girls*).  It was a normal night for **this** crowd.

* Some of you readers will understand instinctively what Zvortyl is and how to pronounce it.
You are the people my mother warned me about.
But we'll have to edge-u-mah-cate the rest of you geeks and dorks with a glittering tutorial on the genealogy
("roots" to you, low-life) of this gem.
Why?
Because this is **Fashion** Philosophy.
By Ronco.
From La-La Land

Last weekend, they were all standing around partying in Paula's living room to loud rock'n'roll, and suddenly the urge came over everyone to have a game of indoor frisbee. Paula rifled through her bedroom closet for her frisbee, but she couldn't find it. So, she went to the kitchen, reached into her refrigerator, and pulled out a frozen pizza, and they used that. It's close enough.

That was La-La Land. And tonight, Bruce is probably going to order a Pineapple Sundae with Rocky Road ice cream for the 27th time in a row. You have to think about that for a minute.
Pineapples on melted chocolate ice cream? Yuck! It's disgusting. The waitrons would always look at him a little sideways whenever he ordered it. They suspected. And he ordered it Every Time. Bruce was on the fringe. MBA by day. Space-case by night.

The van arrived at its destination and the concertgoers piled out and headed for the restaurant. They probably did not literally stumble into Zen-Sun's, but at that point, who knows. They were .....er..... drunk. That's it, they were drunk. They had been drinking. A lot.

Boy, it was bright in there. Zen-Sun's made the mistake of seating them and giving them menus. The partyers looked at the pretty pictures on the menus and that was it, because none of them could read by then. In fact, just keeping a straight face was taking most of their concentration.

There were normal nuclear families from Sloburbia around them with children slurping sodas and chorfing down sundaes. But this group was visiting Zen-Sun's from outer space, and suddenly everything seemed very funny indeed. If they got sundaes, they would have probably taken the spoons and shoveled them into their shirts.

The six friends looked at each other across the table and they knew they were getting into trouble. Their little group didn't fit into this scene, and their predicament was changing from funny to hilarious. Bruce and Clark were turning red in the face trying to keep themselves from bursting out laughing. Amy was just barely hanging on by her fingernails. Paula and Karin started looking at the door and plotting an escape route into the dark blanket of the night if they had to make a run for it. Everything was getting funnier and funnier, and Paula didn't know how long they could hold on. It was going to be obvious to other people pretty soon that these loonies were out of control.

The partyers might have been able to deal with this if it hadn't been for the fact that they were going to have to order. As Paula saw the waitron coming down the aisle towards their table, she knew the Moment Of Truth was approaching fast. They were either going to have to somehow get a hold of themselves and stop laughing long enough to order, or they were going to have to dash for the door like pronto.

Closer and closer she came.
Sooner and sooner that moment was going to arrive.
Try for it or run for it?
Try for it!  Run for it!  Try for it!
She's here!  "Have you decided yet?"

Bruce spoke first, since he was the one who had suggested Zen-Suns and gotten them into this mess.
He said: "I'd like to have a hot fudge sundae."

The clarity and control in his voice surprised him.
It was great.  Solid as a rock.
She'd never know he was on the edge of hysteria.
Clark and the others would be inspired by his cool and they'd be able to handle it.  This is going to work out.
But then she asks:
"What kind of ice cream would you like on your sundae?"

This took him by surprise.
He hadn't expected another question.
He was off-balance, but he quickly came to his senses and ordered the only two flavors he could think of:

> "I'll have one scoop each of
> vorklit and chinilla."

Vorklit and chinilla. Right in front of the waitress.
He thought, *I hope she's one of us....*
She better be one of us. Otherwise, she's going to take the order, walk calmly back behind the counter, and pick up the phone. Is she going to phone in the order to the ice cream company? No, no. She's going to call the FBI, the CIA, the National Guard and the Air Force.

Bruce is frozen like a statue, just having ordered vorklit and chinilla. The waitress has that look of wandering doubt in her eye. She's probably thinking about making that call. But then she turns her head towards the entrance into the parlour, and her glaze falls upon a cool dude coming in the doorway. He calls out to her, "I'll have the same thing as Bruce, but let me have some zvortyl on the chinilla."

Paula jolts up out of her seat and hollers, "Derek! Derek Durban! You guys were great tonight!"
Derek yells back, "Paula! Clark! Karin!"

Now all four of them are swarmed around the rock star, fresh from the concert. They exchange greetings, and Paula introduces Derek to Brad and Amy. Bruce recovers his composure and introduces Derek to the waitress, and she blushes as she shakes Derek's hand. As the others sit down, the waitress and Derek talk for a moment, and then she asks him:
"What's 'z v o r t y l'?"

Derek smiles at her and replies:
"To understand zvortyl, Melanie, you first have to understand vinyl....

"Vinyl was a new miracle molecule
invented in the Beatnik era
of new suburbs
and modern appliances at affordable prices.

"Vinyl was, like, that rubbery plastic mung
they made toys and kitchen floors out of.
At least, that's my opinion of it.
To other people, it was big business.

"Companies used to advertise their products were made out of vinyl. It was a big deal.
They don't do it today. Nobody gives a shit.
But Madison Avenue[1] left us with the legacy of the word itself.
Vinyl.
It looks and sounds as artificial as the rubbery plastic garbage it describes. I mean, if there was *ever* anything on Earth that Mother Nature *didn't* make, vinyl was it. The last thing you would ever see growing in the forest would be a vinyl plant. 'Oh look, Ezmirelda! There's a wild vinyl bush.' Like, it was totally man-made. It was society's debris. Plastic!"

---

[1] Dork translation---the place deception calls 'home'

Paula called out to an imaginary friend:

"Marge, look what happened to Vinyl!
It turned into Zvortyl!"

"Yeah! That's it!" Derek exclaimed.
"Vinyl *mutated*. It became Zvortyl!
It mutated along with everything else
that went from the old mold into the new view."

"Zvortyl is the vinyl of the Aquarian Age!" Paula
proclaimed. "All eras have their embarrassments.
Historians will decide which one was worse –
Vinyl or Zvortyl."

"Paula, you've got it wired," Derek congratulated her.
Turning to the table, he said:
"Now here's how the rest of you can be like Paula and
master this key new concept. Just pay attention as I give
you the word on. . . . . . . . .

"One! 'Z' as in **Zorro**.

Zorro!
The fox so cunning and free.
Zorro!
Who makes the sign of the Z.
Zorro!
Zorro!
Zorro!
Zvortyl.

"Two! 'Vortyl' as in **Vorklit** and **Vinyl**.

"Three! Combine these three sounds:

Zorro. Vorklit. Vinyl. Zvor'-tyl

Zorro. Vorklit. Vinyl. Zvortyl.

And now you can pronounce Zvortyl!
Congratulations! You win a cookie!"

Derek finished. Around the table, mouths gaped open. Saucer-shaped eyes stared blankly into space. No one was sure if what had just happened was real. Everyone waited, but nobody spoke. It was the waitron who finally burst the bubble. She untied her apron, flung it on the table, sat down next to Paula, and said:
"I'm in on this, whatever it is."

Now Derek placed both hands on the table and faced squarely into the group.
"Society and your parents wanted you to believe that the world was made of vinyl, didn't they?" he asked.
A murmur of agreement circled 'round the table.
"But you got away from them, didn't you?" he continued, standing up. "You broke the code. You punched through the fabric of their world, didn't you?"
Paula and Amy began standing up.
"And you found something **new**, didn't you?" he said.
"Yes!" Paula responded.
"Was it vinyl?"
"No!" echoed a chorus of voices. They were all standing now.
"What was it?"
"Zvortyl!" came the reply.
"Are you ready?" he urged them. "Who's with me?"
"Rah, rah, jack me up, run through a brick wall!" hollered Brad.
"Let's goooooooooo!" yelled Derek, and in a mad dash for glory, they all streamed out of the ice cream parlor amid hoops and hollers. Derek ran into the night ahead of them and came back with a light tan van. As it

approached the group from the depths of the parking lot, the sandy colored van began to take on a form, a color, and almost a texture. And then they saw it——a solid coating of hundreds of small white and orange seashells covering the entire surface area of the van, except for the windows, wheels, bumpers, and California plates. Hazy cobalt blue light glowed from beneath the running boards of the shell-covered van, given off by dozens of tiny bulbs.

Seven people collectively sucked in large gulps of balmy night air, and inadvertently held them, eyes bulging. Derek rolled down the window and hollered: "Let's goooooo!" Everyone exhaled and piled into the van.

*   *   *

As Amy sat down, crushed velvet met her skin on the seat. She noticed plush maroon velour also covered the walls and ceiling of the van's smartly-appointed interior. Once underway, Derek reached into his shirt pocket and handed a shiny disk to Paula, who was sitting up front next to him. He said something to her, and she stuck the disk into a slot beneath the dashboard. A video monitor built into the ceiling of the van came to life with the image of a tall guy holding an electric guitar. *That's Novak*, thought Paula. A headline flashed on the screen above the man, and he began to speak.

# Why Offending You, The Party Member, Is So Important To Us

"Here at Zvortyl Headquarters, we call each other names
all the time," the man said.
"We want you to feel like one of the family, so we'll treat
you like one of us.
Be prepared for some razzing.

"Also, you are using 5% of your power.
This isn't some quack theory. It's real.
During Kolinar, you see the other 95%.

"Why be complacent, if you're only using 5%?
Why be so sure that you know it all?
If you're crawling when you could be flying,
maybe you're not so smart after all.

"We are merely reminding you that you are tiny
compared to your full potential, you clown.
We're doing you a favor.
"Besides, I like calling you names.
They don't call me the Mocker Rocker for nothin'.

"So when you write me and send me stink bombs in the
mail, it's okay to attach a little card calling me names,
too. I don't mind. I *know* I'm an idiot, and I feel good
about it.

"And with a little practice, so can you."

The image faded, and was replaced on the screen with the words:

## <u>Who Should Join The Zvortyl Party</u>?

"Good question," said Brad.
"People who collect sea shells?" asked Melanie.
The screen came back to life.
"Rock'n'roll party animals should join the Zvortyl Party," said Novak.
He elaborated:
"The reason I want the party animals is that
'preppie sex' is a contradiction in terms.
You're not going to find that many preppies having blockbuster orgasms.
That's the domain of the party animals.
That's their territory. It's why they're there.
The preppies are out to lunch.

"I wanna talk to the people who have blockbuster, tear-the-walls-down, nuclear orgasms.
I wanna talk to the people who know
the true meaning of the word Rush.
You people can understand Kolinar,
because you've had a taste of it already."

Amy looked at Clark. *The Zvortyl Party is for sex maniacs?* she wondered. *This guy should qualify.*

Novak went on, "Those total fireworks you experience aren't just chemicals dancing around in the molecular

universe, buddy. It's a rush of **Awareness**. It's a wave
of pleasure. Your awareness is INTENSIFIED, big time.
That is step number one. What you happen to be aware
**of** is pleasure. That is step number two. But the
experience is first and foremost one of awareness.

"**You** people are knocking on the Gates of Kolinar.
And always remember what takes you there is Love.
Well, I guess Lust takes you there, too. Let's see, we'll
have to invent a New Age word for Lust. Oh, I know.
We'll call it: 'Love Energy.'
Yeah. That's beautiful.

"So here is mah message to all you thrill-seeking, music-
blasting, nymphomaniac party animals:
Kolinar is like the best of what you already got now.
It's just more of the same thing!!

"People tell you you're just into physical kicks.
Don't let them sell you that jive! I know you better!
You're into *pleasurable awareness*——in a BIG way——
and Kolinar is just more of that!!! It's just *more* of what
you're already into.

"I don't want the people that are out there worshipping
the almighty dollar. . . . .
The straights. The preppies. The stockbrokers.     Your
government.

"Naawww, I want the **pardy** animals. The people into
worshipping **love** and **pleasure**.

**You** are the ones I want!
You people are halfway there already!!!
That's why I want **Y-O-U** ! ! !

"Now listen. Here's how you do it. To get to Kolinar, first you have to know where you're going. I mean, it would help. So rock on, you interdimensional pleasure gluttons. The answer's around here someplace....."

The screen went blank. Paula turned around to the back seat and giggled, "What do you think, pardy hounds?"

"He speak-ah mah language," Clark grunted.

"Thought so," Paula said. "Now try this," and she jammed in some kickass rock'n'roll. Music blasting, the cobalt blue-glowing van sped into the night.

# 3.  THIRD MILLENNIUM

Leaving the city lights in the distance behind them, the van traveled swiftly to the outskirts of town.  Derek peeled off on a small unmarked road that led into the desert.  Large red boulders loomed eerily in the moonlight as the vehicle made its way up a winding hill through the desert.  Suddenly Derek slowed down and pushed a button underneath the dash.  As they rounded a bend, a square section of terrain on the side of a small hill to their right gave way, and collapsed into a rectangular opening.  Derek plowed straight towards the hill, through the black opening, and into a gleaming aluminum underground tunnel.  The van surged ahead down the subterranean passageway as the tunnel opening sealed itself behind them.  In the back seat, eyes widened.

As the van plowed on, Brad and Paula could feel the tunnel slanting at an angle downwards into the earth.  After a few minutes ride, they arrived at a large white gate in the tunnel.  A sentry dressed in gray desert fatigues greeted them and spoke with Derek.  Then the man opened the gate and they entered a parking area, where Derek pulled into a numbered space and stopped.

The wayfarers disembarked from the seashell-covered vehicle and headed towards the end of the garage, halting before a gleaming metal door.  Derek pushed a silver card into a slot beside the door and it swung open, revealing a spacious underground rock chamber about seven hundred feet long. The massive rock walls slanted upwards at a steep angle, joining at the pinnacle of the cave some three hundred feet above. Cool damp air met their faces as the astonished newcomers tramped through the airlock into the underground cavern.

In the center of the room, a white marble table flecked with chips of crystal sparkled beneath a cone of light that emanated from the cavern's ceiling. Standing next to the table was a young-looking woman in desert gray with dark hair and a raven's eyes.

She came forward to embrace Derek, and the two of them performed a secret handshake ritual, comprising three different movements. Derek then motioned to everyone to step forward around the table. As they gathered around, he said:

"Friends, this is Tara. She will be our guide here. Tara, I'd like you to meet Paula, who ran the laser light show on my concert tour last year. Paula, this is Tara. I'd like you to meet Brad, who is a friend of Paula's and plays the bass guitar. Brad, this is Tara. I'd like you to meet Melvin, who sells life insurance, raises sheep, and dabbles in convertible bonds. No, just kidding. This is really Bruce, who owns a bookstore near the university. And this is Karin, she works for an airline. Her favorite animal is a wolverine. Here's Clark, he works at a radio station. Doris here teaches second grade and likes movies, dining out and travel. Fooled you again. This is really Amy. She's a botanist, and her favorite color is green. And this is Melanie, the newest member of our group, and she's a food service professional."

Tara now turned and faced the gathering, saying: "Welcome to our Kolinar Base, all of you. I am sure you have many questions. I will try to answer the obvious ones first. To begin with, you are standing in the interlock chamber. It is a natural orifice of limestone and granite, carved into the earth some 300,000 years ago by the motions of water and the elements. The rock formations to your left are called the Big Buffalo and the Purple Antelope. The temperature here below the surface is an even 67 degrees year 'round."

Bruce and Melanie gazed at the rock formations. They *did* appear to take the shapes of animals.

"Now if you will follow me," Tara continued, "I will take you to the Oracle."

They followed Tara's shadow shape——up steps, a turn, more steps, into a tunnel, past two moisture sealed doors and into a lighted narrow passageway with red rock walls and a low ceiling. A faint odor of unwashed bodies reached their nostrils as they climbed through the tunnel. The group swept forward into a wider chamber, finding themselves in an open space.

Tara nodded to a cluster of children who stared at them from the raised ledge of a side passage overlooking the chamber. Bruce glimpsed adult shapes behind the children partly hidden by filmy hangings. Now Tara swerved left, and led the way down a side passage, turning right into a wide cross tunnel lighted by evenly spaced yellow overhead globes. At the end of the tunnel, she stopped in front of a thick wooden door fitted snugly into an archway. Tara announced, "Behind this doorway waits Diana, our seeress." With a tug, she pulled open the door.

A stained glass mosaic mural backlit by an unseen light source greeted the amazed visitors as they entered the Oracle's chamber. Hanging plants were suspended from rafters in the ceiling by thin metal wires. A musty smell hung in the air. The chamber was silent, with only the faraway sound of water dripping. Rows of stone gray benches covered with orange cushions filled the room. A pleasant looking Asian man was sitting in the front row. He turned around.

"Meet Kevin, everyone," said Tara. "He got here just before you."

After a few moments, a woman in a black dress entered the front of the chamber from a side door. Her face had delicate features and distant eyes, framed by long black hair. She wore a bead necklace, dark brown leather boots, and, over her thin shoulders, a cape-like shawl bearing a silver insignia. She seated herself in a high-backed wooden chair in the front of the chamber. Tara rose and said to her: "Diana—tell us of The Future." After a moment, Diana spoke:

"The first Millennium was from 0—1000 AD.
The second Millennium was from 1000—2000 AD.
The third Millennium is from 2000—3000 AD.

"The turn of the Millennium is an important event."
Her expression lightened.
"It means that The Future is finally here." She smiled.
"Yay!" she cheered.
"City glitter. World harmony. Space base......"

*Space base*, thought Amy, *or space case....?*

"So we gotta get it together," Diana proclaimed.
"We've got to shine up this place
and rock the 21st Century in style
to set the right example
for generations that follow.

"Let's kick it off right
with positive energy, cultural vitality
and brotherhood.
Heaven on Earth is the objective
for all peoples for the Third Millennium."

*Can't argue with that*, Paula told herself.

"Let's say so," Diana urged them.
"Let's lay it down, people.
Let's let every student know
who studies history for the next thousand years
that those people around the Year 2000

were really hauling ass to aim the world
in the right direction.

"Can you get into that?
Check it out.
We're making history
one way or another.

"We can't postpone the new Millennium
'til a more convenient time.
History is taking the snapshot
whether we're ready or not.

"Do you want the People of the Future
to look back on the Founders of their Millennium
and see a bunch of assholes?

"Or would you like them to see a proud people
who overcame their faults
and got their act together?

"The picture History is taking
is going to be remembered for a thousand years.
So why don't we all smile for the camera?
These major family portraits
don't happen very often.

"This new Millennium is the best excuse
we've ever had as a race of humans
to clean up our act." She paused, and then rose and
walked over to a table on her left.

Brad said, "Suppose I buy that. What can I do to help?"

Diana smiled at the party animal, and then answered, "First, get to know yourself as well as you can, particularly your Inner Mind."
*If you have one,* she thought.
"Cultivate the highest quality mental decor you can muster.

"Second, join The Zvortyl Party. Fill out the application form in the back of the room and give it to Tara. We'll help you make that quantum leap into HyperAwareness for the Third Millennium.

"Third, find something in your life that you can be really good at, and do the very best job with it that you possibly can.

"It doesn't matter what it is.
It could be underwater basket weaving.
Just find one thing and do it well."

"Can you give us an example?" Amy asked.

"Sure," Diana answered. "For instance, if you're an artist, you'll want to unveil the very best paintings you have ever done.

"If you're a teacher, you'll want to prepare the very best curriculum you've ever taught for your subject and deliver it.

"If you're a company, you'll want to introduce the very best new product you are capable of.

"If you're a farmer, you'd manage your land so you could raise the best quality of crops you'd ever produced.

"If you're an actor or actress, you'd want to give your best performance ever.

"If you're a waiter or waitress, you'd go out of your way to give your customers the best service you ever gave.

"If you're a craftsman, you would strive to do your highest quality work ever, because things made around the Year 2000 will be collector's items for centuries."
She paused.

"Get the idea?
Everyone pulls together
and we kick this thing off with gusto
throughout every nook and cranny of human life.

"So get off your butts, couch potatoes!
Start acting and getting busy now.
Let's send up a cheer
that echoes for centuries....."
Diana finished.

"And last but not least," Tara piped up from behind them,
"now that we've entered the Third Millennium,
when you're at home, and the phone rings,
don't answer it with, 'Hey, Mannnn' anymore.

"Make it special. Make it new.
Pick up the phone and say,
'Hey, Mannnn, it's The Future!'"

Diana rolled her eyes. "Thank you, Tara," she droned.

# 4. PRELUDE TO KOLINAR

A tall, hearty, barrel-chested fellow with reddish hair and a full beard bounded into the room. Diana and Tara lit up in unison with delight.

"Rusty!" said Diana in a liquid voice, "I'm so happy you could come by."

"Think nothing of it," growled Rusty, as he put one huge arm around each lady in a big bear hug. "Who are our new friends?" he asked, surveying the group seated in the chamber.

Tara told the group, "Everyone come up and meet Diana and Rusty. Rusty is our Base leader."

The party animals came up and shook hands with Rusty and Diana. Then Rusty asked if they had any questions.

Bruce said, "On our way here from Zen-Sun's, some guy on Derek's TV told us about an experience that was . . . . beyond . . . . the boundaries of human limitations. And now here we are in this underground society we never knew existed. Was the guy on Derek's TV nuts? Is there anything to what he said? Is this experience real?"

Rusty replied, "The guy on Derek's TV, his name is Roc Novak, he told you of Kolinar. Yes, it's real."

Brad asked, "What do we have to do to get there?"

Rusty answered, "To qualify for passage to Kolinar, you mostly just gotta wanna have a big, friggin' thrill. . . . . . . That should come natural to you, as it's probably very close to your core life's purpose."

Amy looked at Clark. *Now **there's** a candidate*, she thought.

"Next," Rusty went on, "you have to be willing to gamble your belief system about the way life is, because you are in for the biggest surprise of your life, bub. And you can only receive it with an open mind.

"You may THINK you know everything now, but let me assure you, the world will look very different to you once you're a Kolinar." He paused and surveyed the new recruits. Space cadets. Good material.

He resumed, "Of course, **we** know **you** always have to **act** like you know-it-all, even if you're in a **fog**. But when you saunter up to the launching pad to take off with me, get ready to roll the dice on what you think is reality. Because **you** have **no** idea what I'm setting you up for."

*You're right*, thought Brad, *I don't.*

"To understand why," Rusty explained, "imagine you are a day-glow orange golf ball sitting on a wooden tee in green grass, and Uncle Rusty is getting his trusty Number 3 wood out of his bag of clubs.

"You're about to boldly go where no golf ball has gone before.

"Be the first golf ball on **your** block to orbit the Earth.
Or, in your case, the first goof ball."
Laughter rippled around the room.
"That's what's happening here.
You're being teed-up for takeoff."

"Where does the flight power come from?" asked Amy.
"Well," Rusty answered, "there's ten thousand watts of light that's hiding inside that body and mind of yours.
And *where* it is hiding is the big secret.
The **lost** secret in your case, we are sure."
"Thank you," Amy said, above the snickering.

Rusty continued, "But through the magic of MINDSURFING, we will show you how to tap this extra power and bring it to the surface of your consciousness.
Kind of like diving for buried treasures.

"If you learn the ropes, and do Mindsurfing conscientiously, and follow all the instructions, you'll make it.  There is a road that takes you from here to there, and I've traveled it well enough to know the directions by heart."

"So how do we get there?" Kevin asked.
"First, we have to free your mind from limiting beliefs," Rusty answered.  Kevin gave him a puzzled look.
Rusty elaborated, "You've been confused about what dishwashing detergent to use. . .
You've been confused about what to order on the luncheon menu. . .

And you've been confused about what to believe in.
So you just blow it off.
If you can't figure out what you should believe in, then you say the hell with it.
You believe you'll have another beer.
Besides, half the people out there telling you what you oughtta believe are hustlers . . . .
and the other half are fanatics."

*You can say that again*, thought Brad.

"Well, we've got this problem licked for you now, pardner," said Rusty.
"You can just sit back, relax, and let Uncle Rusty pour his rock'n'roll religion down your gullet.
Just open wide, lean back, and say, Hallelujah, brother, and I'll shovel it in.
You still won't know whether it's right or wrong.
But you know you can believe it.
Because I'm a total moron, just like you.
And then we can be happy morons together and believe the same garbage."

Amy and Karin giggled.  Bruce and Clark looked on in disbelief.
*Now he's making sense*, thought Melanie.

Rusty rambled on, "Second, we're gonna bust you loose from the shackles of rational thought."
Karin looked at Bruce.  *Not a big challenge in HIS case*, she thought.

"As Mankind evolves from Flintstone to Jetzon," Rusty explained, "we go through certain stages, like Neanderthal to Cro-Magnon to Humanoid to Rock Star. The rational mind is a leftover vestige from Man's earlier stage of evolution, prior to the advent of rock'n'roll.

"Frequent listening to rock'n'roll will unravel most of your rational mind — — — — — — — — and this place will finish the job.

"So rock on.
When the lunacy around here starts 'feeling right' to you, you'll be ready for that quantum leap into HyperIllumination."

As Rusty finished, Tara handed out kazoos to everyone, and in lieu of applause, Rusty received a kazoo serenade.

# 5. <u>MIND AEROBICS</u>

After the serenade, Diana stepped forward and announced: "Stand if you want to go to Kolinar."

*I want to go,* thought Karin. One by one, Bruce, Paula, Karin, Amy, and the others stood up.

"Fine," Diana said, "and a motley crew you are, if I might add."

"Yo ho ho and a bottle of rum!" hollered Rusty. "Shiver me timbers."

Diana ignored him. "Who among you is afraid of a direct mind link with the all-powerful Rocco Novak, our guitar wing leader?" She paused.

No one spoke.

"You pussies," said Diana, "you're too chicken to admit it." She smiled.

"Hey, Rusty," she said, "remember the last batch of tenderfoots we plugged into Roc?"

"You mean the ones that got french fried?"

"Yeah. The crispy critters. Where are they now?"

"I think they all went topside," he replied. "They went on to work as big stuffed dancing animals at amusement parks. You know, Goofey, Dopey, Sneezy, Doc. Some of the others went on to careers in daytime television."


"Soooooooo .............Everybody ready???" asked Diana. Then she whipped out a black remote control device from her pocket, aimed it at the left wall, and fired. Sections of the wall folded away, revealing a dimly-lit bay of glowing computer screens. Padded couch seats faced the screens and electronic equipment blinked behind them. Diana and Tara escorted the unsuspecting low-lifes over to the machines and helped everyone into the couches, fastening metallic headbands around each person's head, and giving them hand controls.

Karin felt Tara pull the elastic strap and secure it into the metal buckle. She looked to her left and saw Brad, to her right, and saw Paula. Faint rock music began to enter her mind, making her feel at home, among friends. On the screen in front of her appeared footage from one of her favorite concerts, and the music became louder. She floated blissfully in a perfect state of harmony. At the end of the song, the music and cheering faded gradually into the distance, and the screen changed to a slowly swirling vortex of colorful patterns. After a moment, the colors melted away and four bold words appeared on the screen and in her mind simultaneously:

**Welcome to my mind.**

Her eyebrows jumped.

It continued......

**Come on in. The water's fine.**
**Splish, splash. Slosh, slosh.**
**Hear that? Splash, splash!**
**Welcome to <u>your</u> mind.**

**Your mind is going to sing a song for you.**
**I'll supply the lyrics.**
**You supply the voice.**
**And the person to hear it.**

Warm up time.  Mental aerobics class.
Here we go.  Sing each note in its proper key.  Go!

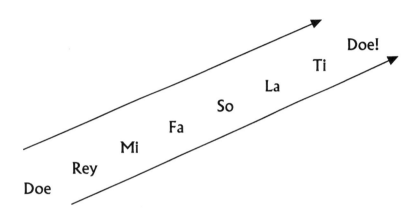

Not monotone.  Your inner voice has a pitch.
Let's hear music!  Low to high.

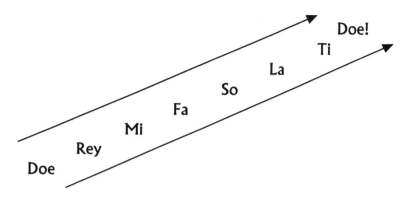

Good. Now, the other way. High to low.

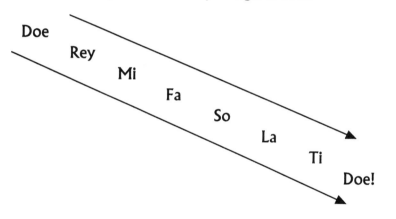

Better!

Now we'll play "All You Need Is Love"
and listen to it.  Ready?
Tune up the band.
Here we go!

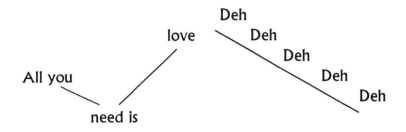

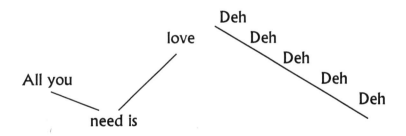

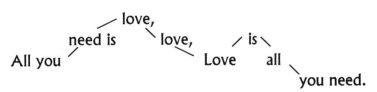

Got it?
The <u>sound</u> is <u>mind</u>.
The <u>listener</u> is <u>you</u>.

**Try it again.**

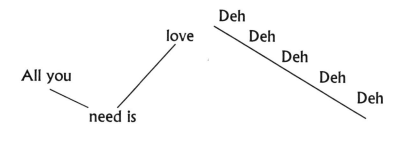

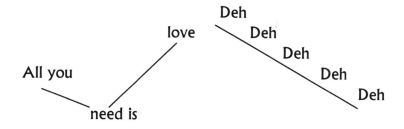

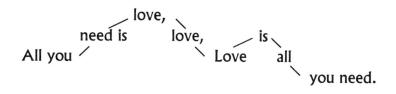

I am speaking to you from inside you.
I am talking to you now
and you are hearing my words now.

To me, both nows are the same moment in time.
The Present.

I am speaking to you
from you.
In the same instant that I form
each new thought on the screen,
you form the same words in your own mind.

That instant is right now, for both of us.
In the moment of now, our thoughts are identical.

Welcome to present time.
Here you are, now, reading this.
Here you are, now, looking at a white screen
with little black characters on it.
The little black characters are grouped into bunches,
and there are white spaces in between the bunches.
You follow the lines of characters with your body's
eyes,
and lo and behold there's a voice speaking to you
inside your head.
And it's your voice.  You are the listener.
This screen links your mind and mine directly.

How aware can you be right now?
Can you be twice as aware?
Can you perk up and double your awareness?
Try it.

What different noises can you hear?
Where are the light spots and colors in the room
you're in?
Wake up, bozo! This is your life!

* * *

The screens went blank.
(And so did Karin's mind.)
In the distance, she heard Diana saying,
"Well, did you get a good workout?"
"Mind aerobics is fun," piped up Melanie.
"What a weird feeling," said Brad.
"Where's my big fuzzy bear suit?" asked Bruce.

Clark stretched. "What now, Diana?" he asked.
"You're going to meet Alamar," she answered. "Follow
Tara. She will lead you to Alamar's laboratory."
"Who's Alamar?" asked Brad.
"You'll see," said Tara, and she opened a side door.
They all got up and followed her out of the Oracle's
chamber into a stone gray passageway which led to an
elevator. A quick ride brought them almost to the
surface. Tara led her group from the elevator to a
winding staircase carved into the earth. The eight
adventurers clamored up succeeding spirals of steps
behind Tara.

* * *

## 6. 21ST CENTURY MATH

At the top of the winding staircase was a wooden door with a crescent moon window. Tara looked through the yellow glass, pressed, and the door gave way to her fingers, opening with a creak. Slowly, the visitors shuffled in behind Tara, entering a laboratory with wooden workbenches, candles, glass beakers, open workbooks, and weird-looking scientific apparatus. "Don't touch anything," Tara admonished them quickly. "You might set off an explosion."

The air smelled like a chemistry lab. They wound their way through a small forest of equipment, stepping over black cabling and through a doorway, emerging finally into an empty chamber 200 feet in diameter and 80 feet high. A huge white telescope mounted on a tower at the center of the chamber thrust its way into the atmosphere through an opening in the rounded ceiling.

Down a noisy aluminum staircase leading from the observation platform clamored a tall bearded man in robes and sandals.
"Aha!" he hollered. "Children of the sun! Even yet my telescope spies your fiery orb!" A broad grin creased his aristocratic face. "Come," he said, "break bread with me, and I will see who among you is a scientist!"

The man led Tara and her group through the far doorway across the chamber into an adjoining anteroom, where a table was set for twelve with silver plates, bronze goblets and candles. The air was damp and murky. As they sat down, Tara explained, "This is Alamar's wine cellar. Look around you and you'll see over a hundred different wines stored in cylinders carved into the stone."

Sure enough, the walls were filled with wine bottles. Servers brought in the food and poured the wine. Alamar held his goblet up and raised a toast:
"I propose joy to our hearts, fulfillment to our needs, and success to those goals which we hold in mutuality."
"Pardy on!" came the reply.
"Now," said Alamar, as everyone began eating, "what would you like to know about science?"

"Alamar," said Kevin, "you evidently have a fine scientific laboratory here."
"Thank you," said Alamar.
"We know science is based on numbers," Kevin went on, "—mathematics and measurements. Can you tell us, now that we are in the 21st Century, what will mathematics be like?"

Alamar replied, "In the 21st Century, mathematics will be taught by people who drive to work with rock'n'roll blaring, and go home and pardy at night, like the rest of us. Our conquest of society will be complete, once we get the math teachers. And we *are* getting them.

"I'll give you a glimpse now of how math will be taught in the 21st Century. Got your calculators ready?"

The servers passed out calculators to each person at the table, as if serving a dessert.
"Here we go. . .
"First, we'll define the problem. Have you ever thought about all the food that you've eaten in your entire life?"
He looked around the table. Blank stares.
"Well, think about it," he said, pausing to let it sink in.
"Staggering, isn't it? You've passed a mountain of meals as tall as King Kong through that body of yours.
And you know what?
You're still hungry.
You insatiable sleaze.

"Now imagine this for a moment, if you will. . . . .
Picture King Kong, the big hairy ape, tall as an office building. And right next to him is a giant pile in the shape of a pyramid. It's a HUGE MOUNTAIN of food! It's a 500 foot heap of popcorn, peanuts, Raisenets, Thanksgiving dinners, sushi, jello, brussel sprouts, green beans, Hostess Twinkies, Diet Pepsi, cheeseburgers, Turkish Taffy, white bread, avocados, tacos, apples, zucchini, birthday cakes, beer, donuts, red licorice, burritos, ice cream, blueberry pancakes, egg foo yong, Rice Crispies, ravioli, and on and on and on.
Jesus Christ! Eat much?? Burrrpp!!

"Fifteen tons of food isn't enough.
No, not for you. You gotta have more.
Oink.

"What an incredible machine your body is.
Not only to pass that mountain of stuff through itself
and survive, but to live off it as well.

"In your present state,
your body is a lot smarter than you are.
Some day, we'll all be smart enough to design
chemical machines so resilient they can pass
mountains of garbage through themselves
and not only live to tell the tale, but survive and flourish.

"But today, we can't design them, and
we can't even comprehend the ones we have.
Airheads are we.
But we do know how to do one thing.
Enjoy them.
So go ahead.
And pass the wine."
Tara filled his goblet. He continued:

"Okay, so now you're mentally equipped to tackle your
first 21st Century math problem, which is:

"<u>Problem #1</u>-- How long would it take the food
consumption of the inhabitants of Alabama to fill the
Grand Canyon?"

"Ready, students? Now calculate. . . .
You take the height, width and depth of the Grand
Canyon and multiply it by Pi (3.141) to get the volume of
cubic space in meters. Divide this by the population of

Alabama to get cubic space of Grand Canyon per inhabitant.

"All right? So far, so good. Now, take the diameter of an average piece of food, say, a Hostess Twinkie, and divide it into the cubic space of Canyon per individual. This subdivides each person's food-space. Then, overlay a red triangle across the north, south and west rim of the Canyon. Take the square root of the hypotenuse, and divide by the cosine of the longitude of Alabama.
Add it all together and divide by five."
"And the answer is:.........."          "Yes........?"
Four hands went up.
"Brad?"          "21.6!"
"Paula?"          "26.4"
"Karin?"          "415.7"
"Clark?"          "33.3"

"The correct answer is:.......21.6!    Brad, stand up." Everyone applauded.    "You get a ticket here," Alamar went over to him and gave him the award, "that entitles you and three friends to an all-expenses-paid vacation to the Grand Canyon," he said, "and a year's supply of Hostess Twinkies!" Everyone clapped.
Brad beamed. His dream had come true!
So THIS was The Future! Wow! Life is gonna be great!

\*　\*　\*

# 7. THE CAMPFIRE

After dinner, Tara announced, "Would anybody like some toasted marshmallows for dessert?"

A chorus of "Yaaaayyy!" rose up from the rookie scientists around the table.

"Then let's go!" Tara exclaimed, standing up. "Alamar, you've been great," Tara said, kissing him on the cheek. "Your beard tickles," she giggled. "Why don't you join us topside for a while?"

"Sure!" Alamar replied, jumping up. "Follow me!"

Alamar led the way to a shiny chromium elevator door at the far end of the wine cellar. At his command, the doors opened, and everyone piled in. A quick ride brought them to an airlock chamber on the surface.

Alamar and his guests walked through the airlock out into the desert. A bright full moon lit their way as the group tramped single file over a path beaten into the ground. Tall saguaro cactuses on either side of the path stood silhouetted against the starry sky like ancient guardians of some forgotten mystery. Suddenly, a shower of golden sparks spurted like a geyser into the dark sky. In the distance, Paula saw a campfire crackling on the desert floor. As they came nearer, Paula made out the shapes of about thirty people sitting on boulders around the fire. Someone began a lively strumming on a cowboy guitar, voices joined together, and a rousing chorus attacked the still night air:

> "They call it ♩
> that good 'ole Mountain Dew,
> *(Mountain Dew!)*
> and thems that refuse it ♪
> are few,
> *(Mighty few!)*
> ♪ I'll hush up 'mah mug
> If you fill up 'mah jug ♪♪
> with that
> good 'ole Mountain Dew!"

Paula gave Karin a dubious look.

Tara led everybody to boulders around the perimeter of the campfire, and the tenderfoots sat down and blended into the crowd. Several more ballads were sung, and then Rusty stood up in front of the assembly, his face lit up like a jack'o'lantern by the orange flames in the black night.

"If you look up at about nine o'clock high over that mountaintop over there," Rusty pointed to the southwest, "you'll see a totally blank patch of sky."
"Wow, isn't that something!" Alamar exclaimed. "Dark as pitch." Chuckles rippled around the circle.
"As Alamar knows," Rusty went on, "I've been studying that area of the heavens in his fantastic laboratory in my spare time."

Rusty threw a small rock into the fire, sending glowing embers skyward. Behind him, Tara was handing out marshmallows, and people began toasting them over the fire.

"Although you can't see it," Rusty continued, "that area of the sky happens to contain the planet Saturn."

"That's the planet with the rings, for those of you who majored in sports," Tara interjected.

Rusty pressed on: "In the 20th Century, scientists believed that Saturn's rings were formed from chunks of ice and frozen debris. However, using Alamar's powerful telescope, I've recently discovered that the rings around the planet Saturn are actually composed of lost airline luggage."

"That's incredible," said Tara.

"I've always wondered where it went," mused Alamar.

A loud moan arose from Rusty's campfire companions, followed by a hail of empty beer cans, which eventually forced Rusty down amid gales of laughter. Tara rose quickly to his defense.

"I think I can clarify what Rusty was trying to say," she began. "Let me tell you about my friend Chloro Phil." The noise subsided. "Before assuming human form, Phil and his pals arrived here from out there," she said, pointing towards the heavens. "Look over there to the west," she said, "about a third of the way up the horizon. See that patch of diffuse light?" Everyone looked. "That's the main body of the Milky Way."

"The central hub of the Milky Way is called the GALACTIC CORE," she continued. "In the Galactic Core, it doesn't take five thousand light years to reach the nearest neighboring planet. It takes an hour on a local commuter shuttle. Many people live on one planet and work on another.

"The reason why there are so many planets in the Galactic Core is because the stars there are real close to one another. Most of the suns have several planets, and there are people living on the planets.

"For people in the Core, it is always daytime, because there are so many suns in the sky. Their body chemistry is attuned to light, and they don't require sleep. Their bodies recharge from photons.

"That's why you always seen little *green* men climbing out of flying saucers. It's the chlorophyll in their skins. They're from the galactic core."

Boooos and hisses erupted from around the campfire. A couple of people threw empty beer cans in Tara's general direction.
"Be careful," Tara said in a voice that stopped the cans.
"They work at the airport," she whispered.
The campfire fell silent.
*The luggage....* thought Kevin.

A tall, slender woman of indeterminate age with long black hair was next to speak. As she arose, Bruce watched in fascination as the firelight danced on her gypsy vest and tight-fitting jeans. Bruce's eyes followed the blue denim as it stretched taut over the lady's long, lean, luscious legs, and his mouth began to water. The woman turned towards Bruce, placed her hands on her hips, and smiled directly at him. Bruce's eyes glazed over. A placid, spacey look passed over Bruce's face, while inwardly he struggled to regain control of his mind. "Aaggkgh!" Bruce gasped. "She's trying to hypnothighs me!"

The woman released her gaze, turning to the opposite side of the crowd, and Bruce regained motor control. Who was she??? She seemed somehow familiar to him, and yet also mysterious. All at once, something in her extraordinary poise gave her away.
It was Diana!

"Earlier today, I spoke with some of you about The Future," began the Oracle, glancing back at Bruce. "Now that we're going to have a unified planet under the banner of the Third Millennium, we'll need to have a new world language. We have created one here, and I will tell you about it.

"We are calling the 21st Century world language 'Earth Tones.' This is because it is more harmonic sounding than prior languages. Here is how it works:

"People in various countries can converse with *others* from their home country in their *national* language— but—when you talk to someone from ANOTHER COUNTRY —or *another planet*—you use the WORLD language. This way, the extraterrestrials don't get confused when talking to people from different nations.

"This new world language is completely perfected and available now," Diana continued. "Although not instantly recognizable by any particular nationality, it draws upon basic cultural sounds common to many languages, making it easy to learn for most people.

"I will now sing to you some lyrics from a song written in this exciting new Language of The Future. See if you can discern the meaning from the sounds."

Only the crackling of the campfire disturbed the desert silence. All eyes were on Diana. She began to intone in a sing-song voice:

> " I-et-day  . . . Epsi-pay  ♪
> O-zen-fray . . . Ofu-tay
> Ig-pay  . . . Atin-lay  ♪
> Uk-fay  . . . Oou-yay. "

As the meaning of Diana's song sank slowly into the hombres around the fire, empty beer cans once again took flight into the cool night air. Diana, very amused with herself, sat down amid the laughter.

More songs were sung and stories were told. As the singing and carousing slowly died down with the fire, Kevin and Amy had sleeping bags thrust into their laps by Tara. Surprised, they watched Tara's silhouette as it visited each of their friends, imparting the same parcels.

Eventually, the campfire cowpokes began slowly drifting away down the path to the airlock, and the eight visitors bedded down for the night under the stars.

For more information on Earth Tones, contact the Zvortyl Institute of Terrestrial Speech by writing ZITS, 119 N. El Camino Real, Suite 200, Encinitas, California 92024.

## 8. DAY TWO

Sunlight touched Kevin's eyelids as he awoke to a desert morning. He heard the sounds of people stirring around him, someone building a campfire. Within minutes, everyone was up sitting around the campfire, watching Tara leaning over a large frying pan in the fire.

Kevin's fork dug into golden blueberry pancakes fresh from the pan, covered in syrup. "A wonderful way to start the day," he said to Paula, who smiled back at him, her mouth full of food.

When breakfast was done, a milky white utility van appeared on the horizon, its movement kicking up a dusty wake along a dirt road. As the van approached, Tara told her tenderfoots, "Here comes Juanita. She will take you back to town. But first, you must make a promise. Hold up your left hand like this." Everyone followed her example. "Clench your right fist hard and hold it over your heart." They all did so.
"Repeat after me....

"I promise..."

                                        "I promise..."

"...never to reveal..."

                                        "...never to reveal..."

"...the existence of this secret base..."

                        "...the existence of this secret base..."

"...to anyone outside this group."

"...to anyone outside this group."

"Very good. Juanita is here now."
A dark-haired woman got out of the van.
"Hello, Juanita. How are you this morning?"
The woman nodded. "Children, this is Juanita. She will be your bus driver for today."

"Is everybody ready?" Juanita asked. The rookies grinned in reply. "Okay," she said, "let's go." The group followed her towards the vehicle. Before allowing anyone to board, Juanita halted and said: "First, a precaution."

A few minutes later, Tara watched the utility van disappear into the distance along the dusty road. It was a 45 minute ride back to town. Once inside the city limits, Juanita pulled off the road momentarily to remove the blindfolds from her cargoes. Shortly thereafter, she dropped the adventurers off outside of Zen-Sun's, where their journey had begun a long time ago, only it was just last night.

Amy remembered leaving the restaurant the night before in a California van, and seeing a guy on a TV screen.
"Hey, Paula," she said, "how much of my mind did Novak say I had?"
"Five percent," Paula replied, "but in *your* case, probably less."
"Probably considerably less," Clark commented.
"Probably you need a microscope to find it," said Brad.

Amy waved them off, thinking to herself, *If I've got 5% now, and the other 95% is missing, I wonder what it feels like when I have it all.* She said, "And I meet the other 95% at a meeting ground called Kolinar, right?"

"Yeah," Paula said. "That whole underground world is all about that."

"So if I'm, like, five feet tall now," Amy went on, "then going all the way to Kolinar—getting my other 95%— would be like being a hundred feet tall."

"A hundred feet tall……" Paula echoed. "That much awareness." She whistled. "Holy Toledo."

While Paula and her friends talked in the parking lot, a pair of dark eyes was watching them. As Juanita drove away in the white utility van, a sly smile curled her lips.

\* \* \*

# 9. PAULA's PARTY

"Look at this," Paula said to Karin, tossing her a piece of junk mail. It was Saturday night, and Karin had arrived early to help Paula get ready for the party. "Good shot," said Karin, as she fished the letter out of the chip dip on the kitchen counter. An odd symbol stared back at Karin from the envelope. It looked like this:

*What the hell is this?* she thought, opening it. There was a yellow flyer inside. It read:

## PLEDGE A LEGION

Do you have any idea how many times you've said the Pledge of Allegiance?
Well, figure 200 school days a year times 12 grades is about 2,400 times.

Can you imagine how deeply rooted into your subconscious that Pledge is by now?
Well, you'll find out later. But just think, day in, day out, year after year, ever since you were a little kid you recited that thing.

Now to achieve bona-fide cosmic consciousness and true world brotherhood, you have to first desensitize the effects of this Pledge. It's not that our country is bad or anything; it isn't. It's wonderful. But it's the subtle karmic effect of the subconscious programming for nationalism that holds people back on the path to universal awareness.

Many methods have been tried to neutralize this programming, but only one method has proven itself to be effective in almost all cases. And I'm about to reveal it to you here now. The truth is, when a person has had sexual intercourse more times than they have said the Pledge of Allegiance, the karmic scale of balance tilts, and the person is able to make much faster headway on their path to planetary consciousness and world freedom. Studies have found that this is particularly true for women.

The Zvortyl Institute of Transcendental Sociology does offer a special accelerated program to help you break free from these deeply-rooted subconscious shackles. Information on the program is free to consenting single female adults over 21 by just sending a postcard to me, Johnny Rockit, c/o ZITS, 119 N. El Camino Real, Suite 200, Encinitas, California 92024. Out of town, call collect. Tune to channel 113 for details.

"Did you read this?" Karin asked in disbelief.

"Yeah," replied Paula.

"What's channel 113?" Karin asked.

"I don't know," answered Paula, pulling out a veggie tray from the fridge. The doorbell rang. "Would you get that for me?" Paula asked.

Karin let in Bruce, Clark and Brad, and joined them in the living room. Paula came in with veggies from the kitchen, saying: "Hey guys! What have you three been up to?"

"Big things," Brad answered. "Yesterday I woke up and said to myself: 'Brad, now that you've hot-rodded your guitar with those sizzling new pickups, it's time to start looking for a more powerful amplifier.' So, I decided to get a Marshall——used, of course. With a Marshall in my apartment, I can do *more* than blow away my neighbors. I can hit power chords that break windows."

Karin raised an eyebrow.

"No, just kidding," he admitted.

"Heh, heh, heh. . . . . Really."

Brad went on: "So I looked in the newspaper for ads for used amps, and I found this guy Rick near the university who's selling a Marshall. This afternoon I went down there with Bruce and Clark to check it out.

"The amp worked great and I decided to buy it. Wow! I'm finally getting a Marshall! This is cool!

"We're standing in Rick's living room, and I start to write him out a check. I tell him I don't have a bank card with me, but that my friends Bruce and Clark here can vouch for my creditworthiness. I turn to my friends to support me in this important transaction, and you know what they say to him?"

| | |
|---|---|
| Bruce: | "Don't do it, man." |
| Clark: | "He's as phony as a three dollar bill." |
| Bruce: | "He'll write you a rubber check." |
| Clark: | "He has a warehouse full of used amplifiers. He does this all the time." |
| Bruce: | "He's wanted in five states. His real name is Mario LaBonza." |
| Clark: | "He's driving a rented car." |
| Bruce: | "He grew up in Bulgaria." |
| Clark: | "And besides, he picks his nose." |
| Bruce: | "Don't let him take your amp, man." |

"This is a good example of Zvortyl Friendship," said Bruce, turning to the group. "Practice it with each other, and your life will take on a new meaning."

"Practice it with me," Paula warned, "and your life won't have *any* meaning, you bozo. Sit down while I get the door."

Paula answered the door and let in Kevin and Amy.

60

"Sorry we're late," said Kevin, "but I had to put a new hot tub in the Lear jet. Installation was a bitch. Took all afternoon."

"But it was such *manly* work..." added Amy coyly, gripping Kevin's arm.

As Amy and Kevin joined the party in the living room, Karin emerged from the kitchen with a surprise. Brimming with confidence as she presented a sure-fire imaginative hors d'oeuvres, Karin set down the tray of uncooked Mrs. Paul's fish sticks on the coffee table. "Breaded sushi, anyone?" she cooed.

The boys went for them. "Mmmmm, delicious," Bruce said approvingly. "It's even better with this," Clark added, handing Bruce the soy sauce.

"Don't you hate it when your apartments change management?" Clark said to Bruce.

"In my experience, it's a signal that things are about to go downhill," Bruce replied between mouthfuls.

"They changed management where I live a few months ago," Clark told him, "and now *lo and behold* we have dogs in the complex. I like having cats around the place, but dogs really belong in houses with yards or woods. And I want the *kind* of people who *own* little dogs—— square women——*away* from me. Get them outta my face. Fussy women who shower twice a day, and their little dogs get manicures and are like, totally artificial and non-animal. Get them outta here. Like, hup, two, three, four. Move 'em out. Pronto."

"Did they move them out?" asked Karin.

"No," replied Clark, "of course not. But all this was a couple of months ago, and I haven't really noticed or thought about dogs since then. But this morning when I woke up, I thought to myself that I really ought to share some of the language of my home planet with you all. So I wrote out a sentence from Zorbitron, and underneath, its Earth translation."

He produced a small white card inscribed with:

Karin studied the card, while Clark rambled on:
"Then I got up, had a protein shake, and went into my office to work. My apartment is on the ground floor, with a large bedroom, living room, and office, that all look out onto a lush, grassy field full of trees and shrubs in between the apartments. I love being surrounded by Nature. I don't need a fucking mansion. This floats my boat."

"It's a good thing you don't need a mansion, Clark," said Paula. "It would sink your boat."

Clark pressed on. "Instead of walking on the sidewalks, people who live at my complex often stroll through the grassy areas in between the buildings. With the advent of the *dog* population a few months ago, however, signs began appearing like, 'Would you idiots please curb your dogs?' as carefree grassy strollers met up with unpleasant surprises.

"As I sat at my desk this morning, I saw a girl out of the corner of my eye go by outside my office window. I hadn't really started working yet, so I turned around to check it out, and besides, I was feeling kinda horny. She was a cute brunette, not too tall. I turned around some more.

"For the past few months, I've been working on reprogramming my subconscious mind for prosperity instead of credit card damage. Whenever I get a chance, I've been repeating to myself, over and over,
>*I prefer brunettes.*
>*I prefer brunettes.*
>*I prefer short brunettes.*

"So this was interesting. Until I noticed what she was wearing. It was, like, this plain blah blue conservative dress that looked like she was going to Sunday School."
"Yuck," commented Bruce.
"And then I noticed she was walking a little dog that had a red ribbon around its neck."
"The *worst* kind of little dog," said Kevin. "Totally fake."

"The dog was on a leather leash sniffing around in the bushes and she was just kinda standing there. Then I noticed - What's she got in her hand? It's like an empty clear plastic sandwich bag."

"That's weird," said Karin. "Why would she be carrying that?"

"And then I saw —— there's something in the bag. She's reaching for it as she's starting to bend down. She's taking it out of the bag. It's a little clear plastic trowel? No, it's a ........... — scooper — ??"

"Eeeeeiiiioooouuu!!!!" squealed Amy.

"Barf Out!!!" blurted Bruce.

"I'm like——dashing for the john," Clark gestured, "ready to blow breakfast . . . .
TOTALLY Grossed Out!!!"

"But what's that got to do with anything?" insisted Karin. Clark gave her the white card.

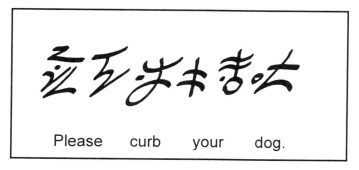

Please    curb    your    dog.

"Oh," she said. "How'd you know that in advance?"

"Interstellar precognition," he answered.

"And you people from Zorbitron have that?"

"Most of us do."

"Remarkable," said Karin. "I never would have guessed, Clark."

Clark smiled smugly.

"I would have thought somebody like Kevin here might be the mental giant among us," said Paula.

"No ESP powers here," Kevin shrugged, "but I've just found a new gizmo that could change all that."

"What do you mean?" asked Paula.

Kevin turned to Paula and said, "Paula, did you know that a new wave of computerized studies on the brain is producing a panoply of tubular mind-altering electronic gizmos?"

Paula stared at him, blankly.

"I'll bet you DID," he continued.

*Oh, no*, thought Paula. *Here it comes...*

Kevin was off and running.

"My friend, Pat, just bought one of these gadgets—
a pair of oversized space-out goggles.
He paid $495 for them.
His friends think he's nuts.
But I say he's macho multidimensional.

"I tried them yesterday. Pat had me lie down on a couch in his guest bedroom with the goggles on and earphones connected to a disc player. He said he'd come back to get me in fifteen minutes, and he turned out the light and closed the door.

"The goggles have these little amber flashing diodes in them. The goggles are oversized, so the lights are actually blinking in front of your forehead, not your eyes. The earphones play tone pulses that synchronize with the light pulses from the goggles. Your eyes are closed."

"So what happened?" asked Bruce.

"It doesn't sound like much, but boy, what a ride," Kevin said. "It was like undulating three dimensional rainbow colored geometric shapes weaving in and out of each other in time to the tone pulses! It was like——," he bolted up, arms waving, "a laser light show with intricate multicolored pyramids of computer graphics rotating around in outer space, glowing with incredible brilliance!"

"Wow, man, sounds like a hot trip!" yelled Clark

"After fifteen minutes, I was in there yelling 'YaaaaaHooooo!' at the top of my lungs," Kevin roared.

"Ride the bull, Kevin!" whooped Karin.

"The next day," Kevin went on, "after paying the dry cleaning bill for my pants, I still had enough money left over to send the goggles a dozen roses."

Amy grabbed a sofa pillow and beat Kevin over the head with it. "Those were *my* roses!" she raved.

After recovering, Kevin concluded, "It's like electronics, man. It's so complex and fascinating. It's like, part of the evolution of Man to the Jetzons.
You know, 'Meet George Jetzon. . . . . . ♪ ♪
     ♪  . . . . His boy Elroy . . . .        ↳
♩♪      . . . . Daughter Judy . . . .        ♩  ♪
        . . . . Brother Bob . . . . .
♪       . . . . Uncle Harry . . . . .        ♩
        . . . . Cousin Tom . . . .'
 Or however the hell it went.
That's where electronics is taking us! Ain't it great?"

"Yeah, it's great, Kevin," droned Paula, "now sit down and shut up. We have some very important matters to discuss, such as how we're all going to pitch in and buy Kevin a one way ticket to Nashville. Please don't sing in my living room any more, okay, Kevin?" Kevin grinned.

"Wait——I found something!" Amy interrupted. "This is important," she said, and she picked up a newspaper from the coffee table and started reading aloud. "It's about living dolls."
**"Press Release,"** Amy read.

**"CHILD, 5, INJURED IN DOLL EXPLOSION
TOPEKA, KANSAS  JUNE 1  U.P.I.**

"Feather Crystal, age 5, was injured here today when a doll she was playing with exploded. At the time of the mishap, Feather was playing with a group of several young friends. None of the other children were injured.

"The accident occurred in the living room of the child's parents, Ray Vortex and Amber Crystal. The doll was one of the 'Brad and Janet New Age Dolls' manufactured by Rainbow Vision Toys, Inc., of Costa Mesa, California.

"Under normal conditions, lime green light beams shine from the eyes of the battery-powered dolls. When the light beams from two opposing dolls are locked into each other, they brighten, and an aura appears.

"Evidently the children had been pelting Brad and Janet with hard rock candies for some reason. This brought about a malfunction in the Janet doll's electrical system, causing it to suddenly detonate. The children were shaken, and Feather suffered several minor cuts and bruises which required first-aid.

"A popular advertisement for the malfunctioning doll states:
'Brad and Janet New Age Dolls! In college, he majored in LaCrosse. She majored in Haiku. He did his graduate work in Styrofoam Technology! She got her Masters in Watercolor Automation! She drives an air-conditioned Jeep. (Available separately.) He drives a cigar-shaped Saab. Together, they cook tofu-burgers in soy butter!'

The other children with Feather at the time of the mishap were Joy Sunflower, Rina Light, Char Vortex, and Dawn Omega."

"Jeez, I was gonna *buy* a Brad and Janet for my niece Melissa," muttered Karin.

"Better stick with Barbie and Ken," advised Bruce.

"Besides, Barbie has more accessories," noted Paula. "The boat, the plane, the wardrobe, the shoes . . . . . . Think of the *shoes!*"

"I don't want to *buy* Barbie..." Karin realized. "I want to *be* Barbie! That bitch has everything."

"Well, until they get the bugs ironed out of Brad and Janet," said Bruce, "you better go with Barbie and Ken."

Meanwhile, Paula was flicking through channels on the tube in the den......

# 10.  JILL'S SECRET

"Hey! It's Star Trek!" hollered Paula. "Come on! Let's check it out." She cranked up the volume, and the familiar lead-in music slowly galvanized everyone's attention to the tube.

As the episode unfolded, it turned out to be a re-run about Jill, a moody space cadet on the USS Enterprise. The program examined the psychological angle of Jill's emotional problems and mood swings.

During a commercial, Kevin groaned, "It used to be that the USS Enterprise was courageously fighting to break free from the tentacles of the giant purple space octopus. Then it got to be about Jill and her emotional problems."

"To some people," Karin answered smartly, "that's progress."

But it didn't look like Bruce or Kevin were one of those people.

As the show came back on, Space Cadet Jill was looking for some way to counter-balance her mood swings. Gradually, she begins hanging out with Commander Data.  Jill feels more stable around the logical Data.  Jill and Data become friends.  After a while, she starts to get a little saucy around Mr. Data.  At first, it's just a wink at Data.  Then it's a hug.  Now all of a sudden, she's starting to *fantasize* about Mr. Data.

"Oh, no!" Paula hollered, "Jill's losing it!"

Commander Data doesn't know what the fuck's going on. He's a robot.
And on the screen, Jill starts wondering to herself —

"........Should I?............or Shouldn't I...?...?........"

"Oh come ON!" Brad interrupted. "You can't *possibly* be serious! Who *WROTE* this script anyway?!"

But no. It goes on.

Now Jill's unlatched herself from reality.
Jill and Commander Data are relaxing in her cabin. Jill puts on soft music and candlelight, sits down next to Mr. Data, and opens her bedroom eyes.

"Omigod!" Paula yelled.
"She's coming on to the android!"
"No! This can't be!" bellowed Brad.
"Stop! Wait! . . . . . Jill, you fool!" Karin shrieked.
"Think about your *reputation*!
You're BLOWING your reputation. . . . . .
Just *wait* 'til people hear you're dating an android. You'll never be able to show your face in a bar again!"

"Later on, Jill," warned Amy, shaking her finger at the tube, "when you swish into Whoopie's bar, they'll ALL be looking at you, *whispering* to each other...."

"There's Jill....." hissed Paula. ".....Dates androids."

"Whoa, Jill!" hooted Brad, "Ride 'em, cowgirl!"

"Ya-Hoo Jill!" Amy yelled.

"He walks. He talks. He's Jill's boyfriend," Clark said.

"Way to go, Jill," smirked Paula. "He's a doll."

Bruce leapt up off the couch and took the floor, a fiendish glow in his eyes.

"Flashback," he began. "Follow me.....

"As a young girl growing up on Earth in Creme Rinse, New Jersey, Jill developed a fondness for electronic massage. Experimenting with new bodily sensations is natural for all girls, but in Jill's case, it went beyond that."

Bruce glanced back over his shoulder at the tube, where Jill was moving in on Mr. Data. "You see," he went on, "Jill knows what all you blockheads forgot——that Commander Data has the android strength of four men, and if she could ever teach him what to do, the robot could jackhammer her straight out of her mind."

"Which is a short trip anyway," quipped Paula, "like you." Snickers rippled around the room.

The doorbell rang. "'Scuse me...." Paula said, "while I get the door."

Paula re-entered the den with Melanie, who was on her way to work.

"Any of you guys ready for an ice cream buzz?" Melanie asked. A chorus of "Yums" ran 'round the den, and people started getting up.

"Wait!" yelled Karin, fiddling with the remote, "I've got Channel 113!"

Bodies froze in mid-air.

"What's that?" Clark prompted.

Running for the wall unit, Paula hollered "It's that wacko channel from the junk mail!"

Paula hit the strobe light, blacked out the room, punched on rock'n'roll and shouted "Karin——hit it!" Karin cranked the tube.

Everybody started dancing to the music, gesturing wildly in the stop-action of the strobe, while behind them, the TV blared:

"The universe is a big place, and it's challenging to understand. But you can start to get a handle on it like this. Go out to the kitchen and fill up a glass of water and hold it up to the light."

Amy ran out to the kitchen and blasted on the faucet. "I got your universal solvent right here!" she whooped.

On the screen was an astronaut in a space suit. He continued, "It should be clear. If it's murky or snowy—— if it looks like a blizzard of little particles dancing around in there——then you probably live in a city. A city whose water system sucks. Write your congressman and go get some purified water. The rest of us are going to proceed ahead."

Amy held the glass up to the kitchen light and yelled "It's a snowstorm in there!"

Behind the astronaut loomed a panorama of stars. He asked, "Okay, are we all looking at a *clear* glass of water now?"

Amy yelled, "No! Our water system sucks!"

"Good," the TV said. "As you probably know, the liquid in your water glass is comprised of molecules having two hydrogen atoms and one oxygen atom. These atoms have a natural affinity for each other and combine automagically, without anyone having to tell them, to form $H_2O$.

"What I find comforting," the astronaut continued, "is that if some outer space dude clear across the universe, a thousand galaxies away from us, opened his refrigerator and took out a glass of water, it would be exactly the same stuff you're holding now. You could drink it."

As the music pulsated, Amy ran into the living room and flung $H_2O$ from the snowy glass into the dancing crowd, allowing her friends to experience the water.

The TV went on, "And not only could you drink *that* water, but you could stop in on every planet between here and there that had water, and you could drink it. Some of the food on other worlds might be a little too spicy for you, but you could stop in and get a drink of water on every planet in the whole universe that had it.

"You see? It's not so *foreign* out there. The atomic elements are the same across the whole universe. Everyone and everything is made out of the same fabric; the same stuff. The elements follow certain rules in the way they combine, like $H_2O$ not $HO_2$. These rules apply not just to Earth but to the entire universe."

Bruce and Karin were running around the apartment, turning every faucet on full blast. The strobe light kept pounding and the rock'n'roll kept blaring.

"Of course, there is a tremendous variety out there. If you spent your whole life doing it, you probably couldn't count half of the different varieties of beers, wines and sodas concocted by outer space dudes. But you could have a cool, refreshing glass of water anywhere in the universe."

"Yes!" Clark roared. "I'll take it! I'll take the water!"

"So why not have one right now?
And get hip to the universal quench thirster.
Water. Take a gulp——it's Springtime!
Share a glass of water with an extraterrestrial today.
If you give him a chemical-rich diet soda, he'll shrivel up into a little pea pod and then explode. And it'll take for-*ever* to get those stubborn green stains out of your kitchen cabinets."

Karin started pounding on the cabinets in the kitchen.
"The stains!" she ranted.   "I can't get them out!"
"Aahhgghrrghh!"

"So share *water* with your space friends.
You like it.  They'll like it.
It'll be good for everyone all around.
Year, Water.
Why not have a tall, cool, ice cold,
refreshing glass of water right now.
And try to remember what it tastes like
WITHOUT the hops and barley."

"We can't remember!   We can't remember!" Clark
howled.
Karin bolted out of the kitchen with all the empty beer
cans, and tossed them on the television, yelling, "We
can't remember!  Yaaahhgghh!"
Paula punched off the sound and lights and they all ran
out the front door yelling "Yaaagghhh!"

# 11. THE ISLANDERS

The party followed Melanie to work in Paula's van. When they arrived at Zen-Sun's, Paula, Clark, Bruce, Karin, Amy, Kevin, and Brad piled in the front door and converged on an empty booth near the windows.

Their waiter, Frank, noticed the party animals seating themselves in his section. "Oh, no!" he said to JoEllen, the hostess. "Not *them* again."
JoEllen stared. "The vorklit and chinella people," she giggled. Frank grinned.
"I'll take them," she said, grabbing menus. "They're fun."
"All yours," Frank said.

"Oh, hi, Melanie," JoEllen chirped, reaching the booth.
"Yo, Joellen," said Melanie, "what's up?"
"Not me, kimosabbe," she replied, "I'm workin'."
"Ice cream, anyone?" Melanie asked, taking the menus from JoEllen and passing them around.
"Mmmmm," said Clark.
"Hey, look!" interrupted Karin, "Isn't that Craig?" She pointed towards a suntanned guy in the entry foyer.
"I thought he was in Hawaii," said Paula.
Karin waved to him. "He sees us. It's him."

Craig joined the group and was introduced. JoEllen took the orders and returned shortly with the goods. As Paula dug into her sundae, she asked, "Hey, Craig, weren't you over in Hawaii?"

"Yeah," he replied, "I was just over there for a long vacation. I even thought about moving there."

"Wow," said Karin, palm trees swaying in her mind.

"I'm finally throwing away my newspaper from Hawaii after saving it for three weeks," Craig continued. "I decided I wasn't serious after all about moving there. Because, you know, it would be like *The Hawaiians And The Americans* thing. It would be like Joe Kahuna would say to you:

'Like, we're the ISLANDERS, man.
Like, this is OUR Island.
And, like, you're STANDING on it, man.
And, like, that's okay, man, that you're here.
But just remember,
We're the Islanders, man.

'And we don't want you messin' with our women.
Like take this girl here.
The one standing next to you.
She knows she shouldn't be with you.
She's one of Our Breed.
So come back with me, Billie Sue,
Back to the land of Irish stew.
Back to the life......of Gypsies!'

"So she went with him.
She had to. It was in her nature.
And, after all, who could blame her?

"Did you know that the Hawaiian translation for 'American' literally means 'pourer of concrete?'" Craig went on. "You have a beautiful, natural, tropical paradise like Hawaii, and what do the Americans do? They come in and pour concrete all over it. Rolling hills, palm trees, everything. There. Now you have a nice Concrete Paradise. What do they think——it will be preserved better that way? Well, now that your island's been immortalized in cement, you can have Statehood. Yep, you're concrete now, so you can be part of America! Isn't that grand?

"Actually, the Hawaiians got back at the Americans for all this in a really imaginative way. Know what they did?"
"No......what?" said Melanie.
"They named every street in Honolulu starting with a K. So when you ask someone for directions to get somewhere, they say:

> 'Sure! You take Kalialuha Street two blocks north, make a left turn on Keleowaki Street, go down half a mile, take a right on to Kaliakali, and then a quick left on Keleolahi, and you're there. Sure thing, buddy. Aloha.'

"And you're saying to yourself, did he say right on Keliokali and then half a mile down to Kelialeki? Or was it Kelialuha?

"And the Hawaiian's saying to himself as he walks away:

'Stupid fucking American. Thanks for the
concrete. Those are the right directions,
but you'll probably end up in Hong Kong.
Have-a-nice-day. Hee Hee Hee.'"

"That's very funny, Craig," said Karin.
"I think you should reconsider moving to the islands,
Craig," said Bruce.
"Seriously," said Melanie.
"Permanently," added Paula.
"Thanks," replied Craig. "I'll do that."

Melanie was looking out the window by their table into
the night. She lifted her hand to pull the red and white
curtains back from the window pane. At that moment,
everyone at the table turned their heads to look out the
window. A seashell-covered van went by and parked
outside the entryway. The conversation stopped. No one
got out of the van. It just stayed there, waiting. Melanie
let the curtains drop. Everyone in the booth looked at
each other.
"Do you see what I shell?" Paula asked.
"What?" said Craig.
"Can't explain," said Bruce, placing a large bill on the
table.
"Nice seeing you again, Craig," said Karin. "Don't pour
any concrete."
"Or tell any more jokes," said Clark, getting up with the
rest of the group.

As Paula and her crew exited the parlor, the hazy cobalt blue glow underneath the van seemed to intensify. As they approached the van, the side door slid open. The partyers looked at each other, eyes wide.

"I have a feeling we're not in Kansas anymore, Toto," said Paula.

She climbed into the seashell-covered vehicle, and the rest followed her.

## 12. SNEAK PEAK AT KOLINAR

After a 45 minute ride, Derek Durban turned the van off the pavement onto a flat, hard-packed dirt road leading into the desert. A low-hanging yellow moon was magnified through the atmosphere to twice life size. After a few miles, the glow of Coleman lanterns hanging over a campsite appeared in the night ahead of them. Derek parked the van near one of several tents at the campsite, and the adventurers disembarked.

Derek talked for a while with three range hands who were seated at a table underneath one of the hanging lanterns. Then he escorted the group into the largest tent. He unlocked a trap door into the earth at the back of the tent, grabbed a yellow mat from a pile, and jumped feet first into a waist-high round shiny copper tube that slanted downwards into the ground. "Wheeeee!" rang out behind him as he slid down the slippery surface on the mat. His fans grabbed mats and followed him into the tube. Behind them, one of the hands latched the portal.

The tube terminated several hundred feet below the surface in a chamber filled with straw. The travelers rolled off the straw one by one, brushed themselves off, and followed Derek through a chromium doorway into a wide tunnel lighted by overhead globes. The stone floor was smooth, swept clean of sand.

After walking for several minutes, they passed through an arched opening into a wider chamber with open space. They went by clusters of people as they crossed the cavern to the opposite side, where Derek entered a narrow tunnel with red rock walls. The newcomers followed him down the tunnel as he veered left, stepped up onto a ledge, and led them through thick hangings of fabric into the yellow warmth of a private apartment. Low tables, cushions, and a platform bed were arranged beneath an orange spread covering the ceiling.

"This is my place," he told them, throwing his backpack down on one of the tables. "You guys will be staying over there," he gestured, pointing to a passageway on the right.

Paula stepped through gauzy orange hangings into the entranceway. The others followed her down a short hall and then into a larger room, about fifty feet to a side. Thick blue carpets covered the floor and blue-green weavings hid the rock walls. Yellow fabrics were draped underneath globe lights suspended from the ceiling.

Through thin hangings to the right, Paula saw, partly concealed, a larger room with cushions piled around the walls. She felt a soft breeze from an air duct, then saw the outlet cunningly hidden in a pattern of hangings directly ahead of her.
"Wow....." she breathed.

Derek entered the room and showed his guests where to stow their belongings and obtain fresh clothes. After the travelers were settled, he told them they would be meeting with a Kahuna, and asked everyone to follow him.

He led his band out into a main tunnel where they passed by knots of people. A file of men and women went by them carrying packs. Rock music sounded in the distance ahead of them. Paula glanced at the openings in the tunnel walls, seeing the heavy carpets on the raised ledges, glimpses of rooms with bright fabrics on the walls and piled cushions. Derek crossed the tunnel to the left, stepped up on to a ledge, parted gauzy orange hangings, and stood aside.

They walked into a round white room with a dozen large thick orange cushions on the floor. Paula recognized Rusty, the hearty fellow with the beard, as soon as they entered. Rusty greeted them all by name, as if he were expecting them.
"Glad you made it back," he said. "Grab a cushion."

As the eight friends sat down, Rusty hit a control knob and the room lights dimmed.
"Anybody ready for a sneak peak at Kolinar?" he asked.
"Yeah," replied Paula.
"Lay it on me," said Clark.
"Hit me with your best shot," added Melanie.
"Okay," said Rusty, and the ceiling illuminated with a huge projection.

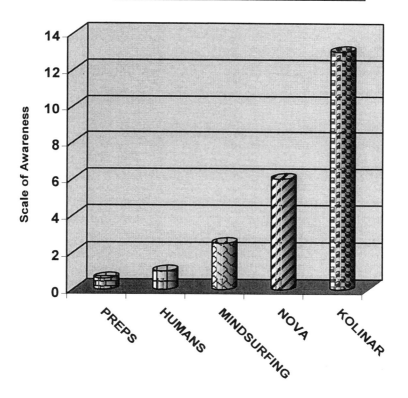

**Awareness Comparison**

Scale of Awareness

PREPS  HUMANS  MINDSURFING  NOVA  KOLINAR

"You can stretch out on those cushions," said Rusty, "so you can see the ceiling easier." As the group reclined, Rusty continued:

"On the ceiling above us, you can see the relative magnitude of several different stages of awareness. Notice the relationship between Mindsurfing, Nova, and Kolinar. This is the escalator outta here.

"At some point during Mindsurfing, you will experience a sudden marked increase in your awareness, called a *Nova*. Webster defines Nova as 'a star that suddenly increases its light output tremendously.' As you can see on the ceiling, you will actually have up to six times your normal awareness during a Nova, and a big one may well exceed that. So here is your chance to be a star.

"But it all starts with being a humanoid lifeform," Rusty went on, and the image above them changed.

"Notice that in normal human life," Rusty said, "awareness is distributed into living and thinking. This is perfectly okay——but as a steady diet, it's limited. However, the stiffs and Preps wander through the maze of life without ever experiencing anything more. Or, if they do brush up against the lower edges of excitement, like when they're trading bonds, it is only fleeting or sporadic. The zombies. But *you* can surpass them."

A new picture filled the ceiling.

"Here's the goal," he continued. "When you are surfing the mindwave, your awareness will rise to the top of the diagram. When enough awareness floats to the top of your mind, you will have hyperawareness——the perfect brainwave."

"Cowabunga!" yelled Bruce.

"Thank you for sharing that with us, Bruce," said Rusty. "Now here's why this is important to you."
The next image appeared.

"During korbit,[1] the main thing that's happening is hyperawareness," Rusty went on. "Your mind and body will be way in the background. Your awareness will fill up the entire stage of your experience at the moment. This can continue for a minute or a day.

---

[1] Kolinar experience

YOU

HYPER-AWARENESS

YOUR MIND

YES JOURNEY
DOOBIE RUSH

YOUR BODY

INHALE,
EXHALE,
ETC.

KOLINAR
SCHEMATIC

"In this and other variations of korbit, your mind will be completely blank. This will be a familiar experience to you if you watch daytime television, or if you've ever walked out of a coliseum to the parking lot at night after a very loud rock concert."

"We're familiar," said Paula.

"Are there any questions?" Rusty asked, bringing the lights up.

"When do we start?" asked Bruce.

"First, you need to know the shortcut," Rusty replied.

"When do we get that?" asked Melanie.

"In the very near future," Rusty answered.

Derek appeared at the doorway.

"Derek," said Rusty, "can you bring these young low-lifes to the west airlock at nine o'clock tomorrow morning?"

"Desert-equipped?" asked Derek.

Rusty nodded.

Derek got the party animals on their feet and led them out of the room. Rusty winked at them as they filed by him and tramped down the gray stone ledge into the walkway.

\* \* \*

# 13. **SIMMER DOWN**

A fifteen minute walk brought the eight friends back to their quarters. Once inside the large room, Derek reached into a storage compartment in the back wall and pulled out sleeping pads for each person. As the visitors got settled, he showed them how to control the lighting and then bid them good night.

Moments later, the lighting was lowered, and everyone was in bed. The room was silent. After a few minutes, a restless undercurrent of activity began, slowly at first, but gradually rising in intensity. Karin and Melanie started whispering. Amy felt Kevin's hand on her thigh. Somebody threw a cushion across the room. Giggles floated up from one corner.

Just as the nocturnal undercurrent was reaching a crescendo, a large white candle appeared waist-high in the doorway. Silence suddenly gripped the quarters. Behind the flame stood a bearded man in robes. The apparition spoke: "I am the oracle of the past. Ask me any question about the past."

Everyone hesitated. A moment went by.
"Who past gas?" Amy whispered.
More muffled giggling.
Brad yelled out, "Have you lived before this life?"
"Sure, Brad," replied the shadow.
"Does it matter?" Brad retorted, wishing the guy would go away.

"Probably not in *your* case," the figure replied. "How much trouble can you get yourself into as a CHIMP, chump?"

The lights flashed on. It was Alamar!

"That's right. If you haven't shredded your membership card by now, YOU are *just* the kind of person who was a JUNGLE ANIMAL in their past lives!" Alamar raved. "That's *you*, to a tee!

"Oook--Oook--Oook--Oook
Aah----Aah---Aah----Aah
Eeek---Eeek--Eeek---Eeek
Err EE Hah--Err EE Hah--Err EE Hah!

"Yeeeiieeuw were a jun-gol ah-ni-mahl!
Jun-gol ah-ni-mahl, Jun-gol ah-ni-mahl!

"Hugga Bugga Hugga Bugga!
Hugga Bugga Hugga Bugga!

"But ME——*Totally* different situation," Alamar went on. "Because in MY past life, **I**, of course, was a King. Your Highness, the Emperor of Molybdemum.[*] Bow down, you chimp.

"I may be a sleazebag now, brother, but that's only because of the *masses of heavy incidents I piled up when I was King*. You see, when I was Your Highness, I fucked up Molybdemum. (A feat few men can claim.)

---

[*] Mo lib de mum -- Aluminum's cousin

And so afterwards, I maintained a low profile, fixing coke machines. It's not because I was *always* a dork. Oh, no. Not **me**. No, **I** was King. Fer sure.

"Now let's analyze *your* past lives so your can regain HYPERAWARENESS, Brad. Suppose there are a hundred experiences you've had in past lives that are causing you to be as spastic as you are today."

Alamar closed his eyes and placed his fingers on his forehead. "I can see some of them," he mused.

"...Like the time in Atlantis you let your bathtub overflow. . . .
...Or the time your ocean liner mysteriously disappeared into the Bikini Triangle. . . .
...Or those campaign promises you made in the Orient to get erected into pubic orifice, only to screw the people. . .

"All these things can and do affect your consciousness today, Brad. . . .
Not to mention being a jungle animal."

"Oook, Ooook, Ooook!" replied Brad.

"Personally," Alamar went on, "I ran my past lives on Zorbitron 'til they were coming out of my ears to get rid of my runny nose, and it was a lot of fun."

"I finally *did* get rid of my runny nose years later when I stopped drinking milk——I am allergic to it, I now know.

So now, I hardly ever blow my nose.
Which is a good thing. Because in the meanwhile,
I've grown a moustache.
And growing a moustache
has transformed
blowing my nose
from a simple, one-step operation
into a complicated undertaking
with dramatic social repercussions
if not executed with complete precision."

"Eeeeeiiiiiuuuuu!" Melanie squealed.
"You're like
Totally gross, man!
Barf out!" she yelped.

"You know," Alamar went on, "I'm sure you already
know all the conventional euphemisms for
regurgitation….."
"Barf," said Bruce.
"Blow donuts," said Kevin.
"Ralph," offered Paula.
"Buick," volunteered Karin.
"Drive the porcelain bus," yelled Clark.
"Pray to the Porcelain god," said Amy.
"Upchuck," added Melanie.

"Very good," replied Alamar. "But how about this one:
Talking to Ralph on the Big White Telephone!
'Ralph? Ralph! Mumble, mumble, Ralph.'

"That's right," he continued. "And, given the furry former lives *you've* probably had, Brad, I'm sure **I'd** have to give Ralph a call if I were ever around when *you* past gas."

Alamar paused for a moment. A muffled sound arose from the corner of the room.

"And to avoid that possibility," he concluded, "I'm outta here. See 'ya later." And with that, he doused the lights and the candle and disappeared.

\* \* \*

Silence finally descended on the darkened quarters, and the adventurers began drifting off to sleep. After a few minutes, Melanie found herself walking through a hazy blue fog in a field of sunflowers. Then she heard a voice. It said:

"Would you like to see the stars and experience another dimension?"

*Yes*, she thought.

There was a pause. She wondered if the voice had heard her.

*Yes*, she thought again.

"Well here's a sure-fire way to achieve that aim, and skyrocket your popularity too." The voice was back. It continued excitedly, "Pull into your nearest biker bar, burst in the door, shove your way through the crowd, jump up on to a pool table, and holler out at the top of your lungs:

'Hey, everybody —— Listen to this !
Only Homos Ride Harleys ! ! !'

"Now doesn't that sound like fun? You'll see stars!
You'll experience another dimension!"

Melanie's conscience sounded an alarm. *Bogus deal*, it
said. *Don't go for it.*
She rolled over in bed.

A man dressed like Robin Hood appeared out of the blue
haze in the corn field. He said to Melanie, "Actually, this
technique for seeing the stars will work in every city
except one. Would you like to know why?"

Melanie was now standing in the corn field. She put her
hands on her hips and rolled her eyes.
*Oh boy*, she thought. *I can't wait.*

She walked with Robin over to a large fallen log laying in
the forest.

"Once upon a time," he began, "there was a pretty blue
and green planet, third world from the sun. It had
smoldering volcanoes, lush tropical forests and funky
little cavemen. One day, a shimmering silver ship
slipped silently from the sky and landed in a cow pasture.
A ramp lowered, a hatch opened, and three exceptionally
graceful spacemen sashayed out of the saucer."

Melanie could see them coming down the ramp. They began talking.

"So, this is the dump Home Office sez we gotta pop-u-late, huh, Dan? Hmmmmmmmmm. Not bad, actually. Pretty place. Nice waterfall. Cool. Refreshing. Not too harsh. Take a breath - it's Springtime."

"Spirits headed this way, Cisco. Galactic overpopulation. Take a number and wait an eon to get a body on TriTon, Gormez, Allistar or Fanemel."

"Biosphere's lookin' good here, Fran. Comin' along just fine. Oughtta be able to support a couple billion with this."

Suddenly, a hearty Scottish man in a Captain's uniform appeared behind them on the ramp.
*Who's that?* Melanie asked Robin Hood.
"That's Captain MacKenzie," Robin Hood answered her.
*Oh*, said Melanie.

Captain MacKenzie spoke. "All right, men. You know what we're here for. We gotta job to do. And I don't want to hear no bitchin' or complainin'. Now get out there, and when I say da *woid*, I want you to

Start **boinking** those local cavewomen!"

Dan:        "Aw, shit, MacKenzie, do we have to?"
Fran:       "Isn't there some other way?"

| Cisco: | "What kinda high-technology ship is this anyway?" |
|--------|---------------------------------------------------|
| Dan: | "Tub." |
| Cisco: | "Can't we just hit 'em with a fertility ray or something?" |
| Fran: | "Do we *have* to?" |
| Cisco: | "They don't even have eye shadow." |
| Fran: | "Maybe they can use yours." |
| Dan: | "Eyelash brushes haven't been invented here yet." |
| Fran: | "They're so . . . . primitive." |

| Mac: | "Ahhh, ya bunch a sissies. Quit yer bitchin' and get out there and start pumping those cavewomen! Go on! Git! |
|------|------------------------------------------------------------------------------------------------------------|

"Sheez. Worst crew I've ever had. Wonder what kinda pre-verts these guys will create in *this* area."

Melanie and Robin walked out of the forest on to a hilltop overlooking a large body of water. They watched the sun travel lazily in an arc across the sky.

"Alright, guys!" MacKenzie hollered.
"That's enough seed-sowin' for today.
Dan! Fran! Cisco! Back to the ship!
Come on. Sheeze! Turkeys."

\* \* \*

Melanie woke up.  It was morning.

"I just had the strangest dream," she leaned over and said to Paula.

"Did it have a van in it?" Paula mumbled.

"No, that was yesterday."

"Oh, yeah..." Paula said.

## 14.  THE DIN-WHANG

After breakfast, Derek picked up his recruits, outfitted everybody, and led them down a busy main tunnel some twenty feet high towards the west airlock.  As they passed an arched opening, Kevin looked through the portal and saw men and women working with stand-mounted machinery in a large, bright chamber.  There seemed an extra tempo of urgency about them.

"What is made there?" he asked Derek, who slowed down.  "Look closely," Derek said.  Kevin stopped and peered into the chamber, watching the workers.  In a few seconds, it registered.
"Guitars," he breathed.

They resumed walking and passed another brightly-lit room visible through an arch on their left.  Kevin saw rows of people seated at long tables filled with electronic gear.  After a moment, it hit him.
"Amplifiers," he said, feeling the chill a second time.

Derek gestured at a tunnel branching to their left.  "Through there and beyond, that's testing and quality control," Derek said.
Kevin understood.
"I want to talk to them," he said.
"We can arrange that," replied Derek, and turned into a side passageway.  He led the way down a rock tunnel which zigzagged back into the first brightly-lit chamber they had seen.  Kevin and his comrades followed Derek

through rows of men and women working on instruments. They heard rock music coming from the ceiling of the chamber. The workers smiled at them as they went by.

Derek walked up to a husky bearded man wearing a red flannel shirt.

"Steve," he said, "I'd like you to meet my friends Paula, Bruce, Karin, Melanie, Kevin, Clark, Amy and Brad." Steve greeted them. "They seem to have an interest in your operation here, particularly Kevin."

"All right, son," Steve said to Kevin, "let me show you what this is all about." He picked a guitar up off the line and plugged it in. "You play?" he asked Kevin. Kevin nodded. "Here," he said, handing it to him gently, "try this."

Kevin took the instrument from Steve and felt the man's presence. The guitar itself was breathtaking. It was like holding a little piece of heaven. Kevin tore off a few riffs. He hadn't remembered playing that well. He looked squarely at Steve.

"How do you do it?" he asked.

"Cosmic pride," Steve replied.

"Can you amplify that?" Kevin asked.

"Sure," said Steve. "First you need to understand the 'cosmic' part." The people gathered around him.

"Some years ago," Steve began, "Earth scientists began transmitting radio signals with mathematical patterns into space, in the hope that the transmissions might be received by intelligent life somewhere."

"As if there was some question about it," Derek interjected. Snickers rippled around the room.

"Let's just say for laughs that there are a million stars in the 'Milky Way' Galaxy," Steve went on. "Scientists say it's more, but really, what the hell do *they* know? They're only 2000 years out of the jungle.

"Obviously, with a million suns, you're going to have a galaxy that's teeming with life. And most of it is going on at the center of the galaxy——the Galactic Core.
That's where the action is.
In Party Town.

"Now *you've* chosen a spatial address for yourself that corresponds to the Moosejaw, Idaho of the Galaxy. You're *Nowhere*, mann. This is the sticks, pal. You're in the boonies with the loonies.

"And not only are you remote, but the civilization around here isn't that good, either."
He glanced over at his workers nearby. "Who can give our friend Kevin here an example?" he asked.
"Topside, now, remember," he added.

"'Godzilla Devours Tokyo' runs on prime time cable," answered an Asian woman.

"Weekends are only two days long," added a long-haired guy in a blue t-shirt.

"Half the world's illiterate," said a tall blonde, "including *your* friends, I am *sure*..."

"The politics are embarrassing," noted a Jamaican man. "It's barely a united world."

"And *you picked* this place, you blockhead," Steve told Kevin. "Big fish in a small pond——that's you. You think you could impress anyone on *other* worlds? Like, maybe, *better* worlds? Yes? Then why are you here in the Little League? Vacation? Wrong Turn?"

Kevin looked nonplused.

"Do you know what they say about us on Alpha Centauri?" Steve went on.

He turned back to his workers.

"Any suggestions?" he asked.

"What happens if an Earthling doesn't pay his garbage bill?" asked the Jamaican.

"They stop delivering."

"How do you give an Earth girl a gleam in her eye?" said the guy in the blue t-shirt.

"Shine a flashlight in her ear."

"Did you hear about the guy who made a million dollars on Earth with Cheerios?" asked the blonde.

"He sold them as donut seeds."

"Embarrassing, isn't it?" Steve cut in. "Well, that's how people talk about us on Alpha Centarui. At least, that's how they *used* to talk about us up until a few years ago. Then something startling happened. The Centaurians began receiving radio transmissions from Earth that all of a sudden made them shut up and pay attention. And that was the last of the Earth jokes on Alpha Centarui."

Kevin looked puzzled.

"No, these weren't the radio patterns of mathematical signals sent by the scientists," Steve explained. "They'd been getting those all along. This was new. It was a strange, mysterious, heroic, pulsating vibration they had never heard before. They didn't know what to call these new transmissions, but the Earth name for it seemed to be something like......." He paused.
The workers roared:
          "Rok-----and-----Rol!"
          "YEEAAHHHHH!!!"

Steve jumped up. "**So**---Go RUN over to the nearest U.S. Space Observatory, BURST in the door, *dash* up the staircase, *grab* those bearded scientists in the white lab coats and HEAVE them over the railing into the reactor pool! Then SMASH that radio transmitter disk that's sending out stupid mathematical formulas and JAM in a disk of industrial strength Rock'n'Roll! Then *beam* that shit up to the outer space goofballs who've been laughing at the mathematics, and WATCH what happens!"

The room sang in unison:

♪      "They'll arrive to pay homage,
          bearing gifts from afar,     ♪♪
♩      just to hear Earthlings play
          the electric guitar."
                                   ♭

Kevin gaped. This was more than he bargained for. He gave the guitar back to Steve, gently, and saluted.
"Had enough?" asked Derek.
"Yeah. Fine," replied Kevin, who wobbled behind Derek and rejoined his friends.

Steve and Derek walked over to one of the workstations to admire an instrument under assembly. As they talked, Steve pointed back to the eight friends and asked Derek, "Where are these guys at?"
"They're about to get the Shortcut," Derek replied.
"I have the film," said Steve.
"Does it work with your hologram projector?" asked Derek hopefully.
"Yup," said Steve. They both grinned.

Derek whistled to his companions to join them, and everybody followed Steve to a mahogany door, which he opened. On the inside, small indigo spotlights nestled in a high stone ceiling illuminated a large round fiberglass table in the center of the room. Fused into the table top was a huge black and white emblem that looked like this:

As their friends seated themselves around the table, Clark and Karin wandered over to look at a bold chromium plaque mounted on the room's left wall. It read:

## The Din-Whang

The Din-Whang is the official insignia of the Zvortyl Party. Its origins can be traced back to ancient Chinese cosmology. Use of the symbol first began during the Vacuum Tube Dynasty in China.

The leading figure of that period, Emperor Mung, proclaimed that the Din-Whang would henceforth represent the Unity of Opposite Principles within the greater Whole of the Universe. Simply stated, this means that different things are really similar if you look at them from far away.

For instance, the distinction between opposites like "night and day" and "calculus and modeling" will become fuzzy if your perspective is cosmic enough. And once you harness the power of this Eastern mystery, Jack, it probably will be.

The symbol is comprised of two sounds:

*Dín*            a loud continued noise, especially a
                turmoil of discordant sounds;
                        -- and --
to *Whang*      or hit power chords.

These two sounds represent the two opposite principles. To visualize how they blend together, picture Din and Whang as two fish chasing each other's tails round and round inside the Circle of Eternity.

The way this works in actual operation is like this: You first hit power chords with a Whang, and then there's a Din while they blast out to the cheering crowd. But if there's a delay box echo chamber, it's reversed, and first there's a Din and then a Whang. If you remove time from the picture - Aha! It all becomes meaningless! The Chinese realized this centuries ago, which is why they went into the laundry business.

The four shapes in the picture (2 fish, 2 guitars) symbolize the four basic elements in the world: Earth, Wind, Fire, and Gasoline. Ironically, these elements also make up the internal combustion engine, which has been challenged by the vibrator, but never equaled.

"When was the Vacuum Tube Dynasty?" asked Clark.

"Around the 1950's," answered Steve.

"So Mung's words have withstood the test of time," Karin mused.

"They certainly have," said Steve. "And speaking of time, we have a shortcut to give you here that will slash the time it takes you to hit the jackpot from years down to two months.

"Such a deal," commented Brad.

"Before you get the shortcut," Derek added, "it helps to know what it is you're getting. I'm sure you all have a lot of questions, and to save time, we're going to show you a quick film which should answer most of them."

Steve dimmed the lights and pushed a black cartridge into an equipment panel mounted in the wall. Above the table, an image appeared in mid-air of tall-masted ships under full sail, slicing through the blue waters of the Caribbean. Behind the ships a voice came.

"In the days of sailing ships and buccaneers," the voice said, "all maps were valuable. But the most valuable map of all was the one that led to a buried treasure chest filled with sapphires, emeralds, rubies, and gold doubloons."

The voice continued: "The Shortcut to Kolinar is like a map leading to buried treasure, only in this case, the buried treasure is you. The 5% of you that is hearing this will understand what I mean when you meet the other

95% of you that's dormant, at a meeting ground called Kolinar."

The image of the ships dissolved into the image of a long-haired man in desert fatigues standing in front of a mysterious-looking temple. It was Novak. As he walked down the steps in front of the building, he said:
"Never before has there been a way for Man to enter this heroic temple so quickly. And best of all, you don't have to clean up your room, your language, or your sex life to get in, pardy hound. Because *this* party is *only* for wanton pleasure worshippers like ourselves. Your stockbroker isn't invited and won't be admitted. Hardee, har, har! Yuk, yuk, yuk!"

The mysterious temple dissolved and now Roc was standing on a space vehicle launch platform. He said:
*The Shortcut to Kolinar is a recipe of step-by-step, practical actions for you to undertake in your life now over the next two months to prepare you for takeoff. It will work to duplicate in your life just prior to liftoff an unobvious and unusual combination of 13 factors that blasted Johnny Rockit right out of the physical universe on July 13, 1969.*

"Let me say that again," he emphasized. "You are getting specific directions for things you can do to make your life a mirror image, as much as possible, of the conditions that bolted Rockit completely out of the physical universe."

"At the time, Johnny had no inkling that these 13 unusual factors were combining in his life in a way that would produce such astonishing results. In other words, he got way lucky," Novak continued.

"YOU can now replace Johnny's dumb luck with a proven roadmap to the stars. This roadmap opens up a secret passageway which will allow you to escape the confines of life as you know it, and drink greedily from the cup of hyperawareness."

The launch platform disappeared, and now galaxies seemed to float by behind Novak.

"Incidentally," he went on, "when you are out of the physical universe, it looks like a big glittering diamond perched on black velvet. The diamond is in the shape of an egg...." He paused for a moment.

"We know that *other* religion tells you that the diamond is in the shape of a chicken, but don't believe them. Follow us. Bag those chickens."

The image cut away to Roc standing on a white sandy beach which, judging by the fine sets of well-formed swells rolling in off the mainland, was obviously in Southern California. Under his arm he held a longboard, and on a blanket next to him was a willowy blonde and an egg-shaped emerald the size of a watermelon.

"Before we begin, a word of caution," Novak said. "Don't go overboard with this stuff. It's very, very powerful. Be careful. Use it wisely. A little goes a long way. Don't be a fanatic. Don't try to set world records. Take it easy. You're not trying to blow yourself into outer space, especially the first time. You're only shooting for Kolinar. Get that first so you know what you're doing. Then, if you still want to fly stunts, go take the Advanced Course. Thanks."

And with that, he ran into the water.

The hologram disappeared and Steve raised the lights. Amy noticed Rusty and Diana standing near the doorway. "If you have any questions," she heard Steve say, "raise your hand." Hands went up around the table.

"Good," Rusty spoke up from the doorway. "We'll answer them all outside. Let's go."

"Welcome back," Diana added, as the desert-clad figures rose to their feet. "Are you all ready?"

Heads nodded in assent. With that, the eight friends followed Rusty and Diana out of the room, a few paces down a hallway, and out the west airlock.

## 15. **SHORTCUT TO KOLINAR**

The ten hikers set off into the desert chaparral in a westerly direction. The sun shone overhead out of a clear azure blue sky. Kevin felt the cool morning air as his boots crushed down small rocks in the earth.

"Where does the shortcut begin?" he asked.

"The first part of the shortcut is Mindsurfing," Diana said. "Like tennis, golf, or disco, the more you do it, the better you get. . . . .
So practice your mindsurfing every day. . . .
And disco the night away . . . . hey, hey, hey!"
Kevin groaned.

"Why bother to get good at it?" asked Brad.

"Because we're gonna put you on a great big brainwave, pardner," Diana replied.
"A wave like you've never rode before.
And if you're like, A Number One Klutz Mindsurfer, you're gonna keep falling off.
And you'll get the Goob Gremmie Dweeb Award for Splashy Wipeouts,
while the rest of us eat bon-bons and travel to Mars.

"But if you're a good mindsurfer,
and you keep your balance on that wave,
you're in for the thrill of a lifetime.

"So you want to get the hang of mindsurfing, now,

while you're still on land.
Get good at it.  Follow the directions.
Throw yourself into it.  Every minute you invest in practice now will pay dividends later during your korbit."
Diana finished, and the trail swerved north.

The path now turned up a long, sloping hill.  The hikers tramped upwards past tall saguaro cactuses with bright yellow blossoms, and prickly shrub bushes with lavender flowers.  Karin noticed how green everything was.

Rusty pointed to a field below them at the bottom of the bluff towards the east.  The field was surrounded by a natural corral of boulders.  Thick bushes covered its perimeter, camouflaging the boulders.

"The second part of the shortcut is desire," said Rusty.
"This part should be easy.
All you have to do is to want an electrifying thrill.
If you're a thrill-seeking, music-blasting,
nymphomaniac party animal like us,
this should be right up your alley.

"You gotta *want* the thrill.
You gotta be hungry for an incredible thrill.
Are you?"
Karin grinned at Bruce.  Bruce leered back.
Paula's eyes had a wild look.

Rusty faced the group, saying, "Are you smiling?
Does this sound like fun?

You have *no* idea where I'm taking you,
but when you get there,
you're going to drool."
Diana giggled.

"Now look," Rusty went on. The shortcut is fast, very fast, but it still requires some work on your part. Your fairy godmother isn't going to wave a magic wand over you while you sit on the couch eating potato chips, and then suddenly Kolinar will rain down on you.

"You are going to have to study the instructions, do the exercises, mindsurf daily, and concentrate, concentrate, concentrate. But boy, will the results be worth it! If you go all the way, you will have the greatest thrill of your life."

As the hiking party neared the top of the ridge, they sighted a long downhill slope with rock walls rising up on either side, forming a canyon. At that moment, an enormous crow flew over them.

Rusty spoke again. "The third clue in the shortcut is self-control," he said. "There are two lions guarding the Gates of Kolinar. One is the Lion of Distraction, and the other is the Lion of Reason. Many people fail to make it past these powerful guardians. But YOU will be able to pass through if you follow the path exactly."

"How do we do it?" asked Clark.

"Well, the Mindsurfing Course will dismantle your Lion of Reason," Rusty answered.

"Along with your sanity, we are sure," Diana interjected.

"But you will still have to wrestle with the Lion of Distraction," said Rusty. "To win this match, you must have something called 'self-control.'" He elaborated:

"If you are an avid party animal, self-control may be a new concept for you. It means following your will instead of your whims. Remember it on your voyage.

"When you begin your liftoff, you will start mindsurfing. In the early stages of liftoff, you may feel like pursuing other diversions instead of mindsurfing. *If this happens to you*, and it may, you will need to have the self-control at that moment to continue doing what you are supposed to do.

"Once your liftoff reaches korbit, mindsurfing becomes a breeze, and the real fun begins. You will only really need self-control to get yourself launched to begin with.

"You have 60 days to practice mindsurfing. If you're conscientious at it, *even you* can develop enough self-discipline in two months of mindsurfing to hit Kolinar, no sweat."

"How much self-control do we need?" Melanie asked.

"If you can force yourself to do fifteen minutes a day of mindsurfing for sixty days," answered Rusty, "you will be strong enough to vanquish the Lion of Distraction, and stride triumphantly through the Gates of Kolinar."

As the hiking party descended into the canyon, they passed by some water in shallow pools. Occasionally, Karin could hear tiny lizards darting through the desert underbrush. On her right side, Karin could see a very large shallow cave near the top of the ravine walls. It looked like a balcony had been carved out of the white sandstone rock. Karin peered up and down the sides of the canyon as they walked along. She became immersed in the richness of color in the rock wall. There were specks of every conceivable hue and patches of light moss or lichen in every rock.

"What's the fourth part of the shortcut?" Clark asked.

"Your environment," replied Diana. "You must be in control of your immediate environment when you get korbited," she explained. "Situate yourself somewhere that is free of any external distractions, where you can concentrate without interruption. You don't need any external distractions. You will have enough internal ones." Diana noticed Rusty grinning at her.

"Chose a perfectly quite place for your korbit," she went on. "Make sure you will not be disturbed by pets, traffic, phones, TV, or other noises. Natural sounds are okay.

"If you can arrange to get korbited away from home, in an environment you have control of, it will work in your favor. Check into a posh resort, or go to the country, or stay at a friend's house."

"If you stay with a friend," added Rusty, "make sure they understand beforehand what you are doing. Ideally, it should be someone else who is also a party member."

"While we favor away-from-home korbits," Diana continued, "home korbits are also possible, and sometimes the results are very good. Home korbits work best with people who live by themselves. If you live with others, go someplace else to get korbited.

"Both indoor and outdoor launchings are possible. However, indoor korbits usually provide the greatest measure of control over the environment. Your external environment must be under control for you to leave it behind. For this reason, indoor korbits are preferred.

"The only outdoor launchings you should even consider are natural environments in the country, and then only at night. With a full set of stars out, an outdoor korbit can be spectacular."

"And with meteor showers, it can be out of this world," Rusty added.

"However, outdoor korbits are more tricky," Diana noted. "If you are going to attempt one, see me or Rusty for a special set of instructions to help you pull it off."

Diana brought the expedition to a halt and everyone sat down to rest in the shade of an overhanging cliff.

Looking up at the perpendicular walls of the canyon, Brad felt a weird sensation. The walls were hundreds of feet high. The sun was almost overhead, slightly towards the southwest. Diana told everyone to open their water packs, and to drink sparingly. While they rested, she spoke:

"The fifth element of the shortcut is collaborators," Diana said. "Since you are fortunate enough to be on a Kolinar Base, you can avail yourself of the invaluable assistance the Base people can provide to you in the exciting adventure you are embarking upon. On the Mindsurfing Course at the Base, you will receive personal coaching by the experts to help you prepare for your launch. You will undoubtedly also meet others like yourself at the Base who are into wild thrills and rock'n'roll."

"YaaaHooo!" howled Clark, his cheer echoing of the canyon walls. Diana smiled.

"All korbits are done with the Mindsurfer and a Navigator who provides direction," she continued. "We will talk more about Navigators later on. Some people also elect to have a third companion around. If you do, it should be someone in the background, who will fulfill your requests without imposing any demands on you. And they should obviously know what is going on.

"Couple korbits are possible, and they are wonderful experiences. They usually work best when one person in the couple is already a Kolinar. The shortcut for double korbits is a little more complex. If you are interested in double korbits, you can see Rusty or me later."

"Unless you are doing a double korbit," Rusty interjected, "the companion you choose for company, if any, should be someone else besides your 'Main Squeeze.' A neutral friend has none of the distracting power of a lover."

"If you do not happen to be in a relationship," Diana added," you can still get korbited. In fact, it will even tend to work in your favor, as you will have fewer Earthly ties to cast off when you launch."

Diana drank from her water pack. Rusty began talking. "The sixth piece of the shortcut has to do with your life status," he said. "When you climb up the ladder of awareness to Kolinar, you're going to be saying 'bye-bye' to your terrestrial life for a little while. You're going to be letting go of your life situation on Earth."

Diana finished drinking. "The happier your life is," she said, "the easier it will be for you to let go of it. Therefore, to get korbited, your life has to be going well."

"Does your life does have to be perfect in every way to get korbited?" asked Melanie.

"No," replied Diana. "You just have to be basically happy. Ideally, your life situation should be exhilarating. But as long as your life situation is at least good, you can still get korbited."

"You can even get korbited in the face of small problems, or minor difficulties," added Rusty. "However, you will get the most mileage out of your korbit if you come into it with the least amount of attention on your daily life. This is because the experience of Kolinar has nothing to do with your present situation. It's more cosmic. It's about you, not about your life. Which is a good thing, considering the sleazy life you probably have."

Brad and Amy made mooing noises. Paula rolled her eyes.

A dusty brown jackrabbit ran out from underneath the brush across the trail. Rusty took this as a signal and rallied his companions to their feet. The hikers continued along the trail as it wound up out of the canyon and around to the northwest. They passed desert shrubbery with occasional green mountain bushes and Joshua trees as they climbed.

After they had walked for a way, Rusty resumed talking. "The seventh secret is travel," he said. "Any travel to new and unfamiliar places prior to liftoff will help you. This is because the novelty of being in an unfamiliar environment pulls your awareness out of *thought* and into *present time*. Present time is where the action is in the korbit game. So travel is good.

"If you have relocated recently prior to your korbit, it will work in your favor. If not, travel is even more important.

Try to go somewhere new before your korbit. You don't have to spend two months in Europe, like I did, but you should definitely GO somewhere, even if it's just for the weekend. The change of scenery will refresh you, and detach you from your daily life. Even travel you have done up to three years ago will work for you in your korbit. Travel is important. GO!"

"Does this hike count as travel?" Amy asked, as she traversed a steep part of the trail.
"No, it counts as aerobics," Karin puffed from behind her.

Diana smiled. "The eighth part of the formula is time," she said when they reached the top of the crest. "Select a time of day for your korbit that is best suited to you. If you are a morning person, get korbited in the morning. If you are a night person, get korbited at night."

"If you are schizophrenic, get korbited in the afternoon," Rusty suggested.

"Thanks, Rusty," said Diana. She resumed, "If you are not sure what your best time is, launch at night. Remember that most rock concerts are held at night. And also, many people think the still of the night provides the most distraction-free environment for consciousness exploration."

"If you opt for a late-night korbit," Rusty added, "be sure to get extra sleep the day before."

Diana went on: "Make sure you have no plans to do anything on the day following your korbit. Having this buffer day will make your 'daily-life-consciousness' easier to let go of while you are in korbit.

"Plan to spend the day before and the day after your korbit by yourself, or with just your korbit companion. You can go out and do things, but no parties and no battling dinosaurs," Diana concluded.

"Take the day before liftoff as a personal vacation day for yourself," said Rusty. "Do whatever you want—go windsurfing, hiking, swimming, sailing, play music, go to a restaurant, go shopping, go sightseeing, or whatever. Then take the day after your korbit off, too."

He took a stick and drew in the red dirt:

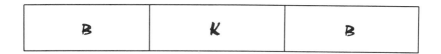

"The 'B' is for Buffer Day," he said, "and the 'K' is for Korbit Day. Having these two buffer days will allow you to smoothly phase out of your life, get korbited, and then smoothly re-integrate into your life. If you are planning to get korbited over a weekend, make it a three-day weekend. This is important. You deserve the best."

"Two buffer days are the minimum requirement," Diana added. "If you can manage a week before and a week after, go for it."

Then Diana said it was time to eat the food in their packs. They sat down on some boulders overlooking the high desert plateau. As he opened his pack, Kevin felt the warm sun as it reached the height of its arc directly overhead. From the plateau, he could see several large black crows circling over the desert plain below.

As they were eating, Diana said, "The ninth part of the shortcut is about your body energy or 'tone.' Having your body in the best possible overall shape will work to your advantage in your korbit. This includes diet, exercise, nutrition, grooming, and minimum pollution. However, you are going to have to knock off any strenuous physical exercises like workouts for a month before your korbit, and at least a week after."

"I am sure you are sorry to hear this," said Rusty.
"What?" cried Karin. "No aerobics??"
"No lifting barbells?" yelped Bruce.
"Yup," snickered Rusty.
"GeeeWhizzz," groaned Paula.
"Why?" asked Melanie.

"Because strenuous exercise pushes your consciousness into your body," Diana answered. "This is good, and it's why it benefits your body, but during korbit, we will be pulling your awareness out of your body and into your head. This will be easier to do if you haven't exercised for a few weeks. So knock off the exercise for a month, and we'll get those lime green light beams shining out of your eyes."

The hikers finished eating and started a downward descent off the high desert plateau. The trail wound around to the northeast. Ahead of them in the distance, a wall of lava mountains rose majestically off the desert floor. The sun was lower on the horizon now and shone on the western face of the mountains, tinting their redness with a dazzling array of yellow reflections.

The view to the west was impressive. Bruce could see a vast area of low hills leading into the desert plain. He realized that they had been traveling in a huge circle.

"What should you wear for korbit?" Paula asked.

"Well, Paula," said Rusty, "that skin-tight leopard skin bodysuit that Brad says you normally prance around in will have to be put aside for loose-fitting attire during your korbit."

Paula thumbed her nose at Brad.

"Tight clothes enhance your awareness of your body, which is normally good," Diana added, and her eyes brushed Bruce's face. "But with korbit we are going in the other direction—to your head. It is possible to get korbited in tight clothes, but only the experts can do it, not you, so forget it for now. That's clue number ten." Paula seemed satisfied with the answer.

"As long as we're talking about body awareness," Diana continued, "we might as well cover sex, too. Rule number eleven is that there are no rules about sex and korbit, so go ahead and do whatever you normally do."
"But knock off the whips and chains," said Rusty.
Diana ignored him. "Sex puts life energy into the body," she continued, "but it also releases it back out again. You should be satisfied, not horny, when you go to launch. Like the rest of your life, you will be leaving this area behind for a little while."

The trail was bringing the group back around into familiar territory. Clark noticed a formation of cholla bushes around a shallow pool he had seen early that morning. The late afternoon wind had picked up and was rustling the desert underbrush. "What's the last part of the shortcut?" he asked.

"There is a bit more," replied Diana. "Food and rest are the twelfth secret," she said. "We believe in good nutrition, but we can't say that it will dramatically increase your chances of having a great korbit."
"People have gotten korbited on burgers and fries," added Rusty.
"Eat whatever seems right to you to put your body in the best shape," said Diana. "This will vary for different people."

"Rest, on the other hand, is absolutely essential," noted Rusty. "Get as much sleep as possible before your korbit. You need to be at your maximum alertness for Kolinar."

Ahead of him in the distance, Bruce could see the trailhead where their hike began.

"The final piece of the formula is consciousness," said Rusty. "Rockets need fuel to escape gravity, and you will have to alter your consciousness for your korbit."

"We recommend altering your consciousness by taking a two week vacation to Tahiti," Diana explained.

"In case you can't afford this right now, we hear the ice cream is pretty good at Zen-Sun's...." said Rusty.

Bruce pondered this for a moment. "It is," he replied, "if you don't shovel it into your shirt."

"Zvortyl," responded Diana with a wink.

\* \* \*

# 16. BACKSTAGE

After re-entering the airlock and riding the elevator to the underground level, the hikers went back to their quarters to wash off the trail dust. Later that evening after dinner, the day hikers met Rusty again. This time, he led them off in an unfamiliar direction, eventually arriving in a cool, damp subterranean cavern. Amy noticed eerie rock formations extending upwards some three hundred feet.

"Doesn't that rock look like a buffalo?" she wondered out loud.

"Hey!" exclaimed Bruce. "That's the Big Buffalo!"

"And there's the Purple Antelope!" echoed Clark.

The friends quickly realized they were standing in the interlock chamber where they had first met Tara the night they arrived.

"There's the airlock!" yelled Brad.

Rusty took them through the gleaming metal doors into the underground parking lot, where a milky white utility van waited. While Paula and her friends climbed into the van, Rusty and the driver spoke in low tones.

"No blindfolds this time, Juanita," Rusty said with a smile, and moments later, the van disembarked.

The white van climbed upwards through a shiny aluminum tunnel. As they neared the surface, a door opened ahead of them automatically, and sealed itself behind them as the van sped out into the desert night.

An hour later, they were parked behind the coliseum downtown, in the V.I.P. area. Juanita led her passengers through the stage entrance into the building. Ahead of her, under the bright lights of the coliseum, Amy could see a road crew setting up equipment on the stage. Juanita veered to the left and they followed her up a staircase and through a door into a large, dimly-lit room. About fifty people were sitting on the smooth cement floor on orange cushions.

At the front of the room was a slightly elevated platform cluttered with amplifiers, cables and guitars. A lanky guy was sitting on a wooden stool on the platform, taking questions from the people in the room. Behind him, several guys were working on the equipment. A reporter holding a notepad stood up and asked a question.

"Roc, will you be playing anywhere in the Southern Hemisphere on this tour?"

"No, not this time."

"One more question, if I may. As a philosopher, would you care to comment on why we haven't seen any world-class civilizations spring up yet in the Southern Hemisphere on Earth?"

Novak hesitated for a moment. Then he said,

"That's easy. It's because the people there are upside down."

"Thank you," the reporter said, and took his seat.

A stocky boy with short hair stood up next and asked:

"Roc, what kind of food do androids eat?"

Roc replied, "Androids eat plastic bananas, wax grapes, those cardboard display desserts in restaurants, and every once in a while, they blow themselves to jello."

He paused, and then elaborated.

"They prefer the firm, rubbery jello. You know, the kind that if you threw a square green block of it down against a table, it would bounce back into your hand in one piece. You know——the kind they serve in high school cafeterias. That's what they like."

A girl with blonde hair wearing a black t-shirt got up. She asked, "Why was *Kolinar* written in Phoenix?"

Novak answered, "Because Johnny Rockit couldn't find Lost Angeles."

A tall guy with glasses and long hair asked,
"Is there a hidden meaning to *Kolinar*?"

"You mean the book?" Roc asked.

"Yeah," the kid replied.

Roc said, "Okay. . . . . The answer is Yes. . .
In fact, underneath the surface meanings of the words on the pages, college professors will discover a street map of Philadelphia."

A young girl stood up and asked, "How do we know we can trust you?"

Roc responded, "Because I can play the electric guitar."

Another girl got up and asked, "Have you ever been in love?"

"Why, sure," Roc replied.

"Tell us about it," the girl urged him.

"Yeah....!" echoed a chorus of female voices in the room.

"Okay," Roc yielded. "It all began in Europe, in a Youth Hostel. For those of you who don't know, a Youth Hostel is a franchised boarding house where kids stay who are on bicycling excursions. You have to be riding a bicycle to get in. Kinda weird, huh? They're big in Europe.

"Now I don't want to give American Youth Hostels a bad name by mentioning them in this room, because they are a wonderful organization. And they could attract a lot more punk rockers by changing their name to American Youth Hostiles. And they could get some grunge rock'n'roll for their theme song, like:

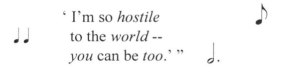

> ' I'm so *hostile*
> to the *world* --
> *you* can be *too*.' "

Booos and catcalls arose from the listeners.

"Just kidding," Novak said. "For any of you who don't know, AYH sponsors bicycle-oriented excursions for kids to various countries. Which is where I met Jeff Judson one summer in Europe. He was an aspiring artist from Philadelphia, and I was a high school rock star from Long Guy Land. We were in a group of kids, led by one big college kid, and we were bicycling from Amsterdam to

Geneva.[1] It was a blast. We bicycled with our group for a month and then hitchhiked on our own for another month. One day we bumped into these kids Mark and Steven from Jeff's high school, and got a ride with them from Munich to Paris. Then we stayed with friends of my parents and they took us all over central Germany. Yeah! Way to go!

"A couple of months after we got back from Europe, I drove down to Philadelphia from Long Guy Land to visit Jeff with one of the guys in my band, Ron Valenti. On the agenda was a rock concert and a rendezvous with my secret heartthrob, Preppy Princess Deborah Fenton, who also lived in Philly.

"Ron Valenti and I have been together in bands for a long time," Novak continued. "Hey, Ron!" he called to one of the guys back stage. An olive-skinned man with an angular jaw came out from behind an amplifier.

"At the time," Novak went on, "Ron and I were high school rock stars who had just applied to Harvard. We thought we were hot shit."

The two men grinned at one another.

"Our rejection slips were in the mail," said Valenti.

Roc said, "Deborah Fenton was the kind of girl who would walk into a crowded living room full of parents talking, and suddenly you could hear a pin drop."

"And it wasn't her mouthwash, either," added Valenti.

---

[1] Places in Europe.

Roc continued, "Valenti had met Deborah when she came to hear our band practice in his basement, so he knew what we were getting into. The worst thing about Deborah, though, was that her S.A.T. scores were higher than mine."

Valenti explained, "For you *gronks* who majored in ath-a-let-ick com-pa-tish-un, you *twits* who majored in home eccch, and you *loadies* who majored in drugs, S.A.T.s are the tests you take to get into college."

Catcalls arose from the audience. "What is reality?!?" someone yelled.

"Anyway," Novak went on, "Ron and I had never been to Philly before, but we found Jeff Judson's house pretty easily. He lived in a middle-class suburban neighborhood like us, only the houses were older and the trees lining the street were bigger. Ron pulled his big red second-hand Oldsmobile into Jeff's driveway and we grabbed our bags and got out.

"Mrs. Judson warmly greeted us and welcomed us into their comfy home where we'd be staying...."
"....In the basement," interjected Ron Valenti.
"We seemed like such *nice* boys," said Rocco.
"...Little did she know..." added Ron.

"The next night," Roc continued, "Deborah and the three of us met at the rock concert downtown. As I introduced her to Jeff, I noticed how her long brown hair cascaded over the blue silk India blouse that complimented her crystal eyes. She had on leather boots under a matching skirt and jacket outfit decorated in a colorful embroidered pattern. She was overdressed for the concert, but what the hell, she was a Preppy Princess."

"And you were buying it, big time," said Ron.
Rocco nodded. "This girl sent me into the ozone layer," he said. "Just putting my arm around her as we sat there listening to the music was an electrifying thrill."
Valenti grinned.

"Being just a young lad at the time," Roc continued, "the subject of Female Anatomy was filled with mystery and fascination for me. Actually, come to think of it, that hasn't changed much. But anyway, as it turned out, holding hands was the biggest thrill that fate had in store for me from Deborah Fenton. Except, that is, for the next day."
Ron Valenti guffawed. They both grinned.

Valenti explained, "Deborah had invited the three of us to stop by her house, so early the next afternoon, we made our way over from Jeff's house to that part of town. I followed the directions she had given me through her neighborhood, and I pulled up in front of this huge, four story Victorian mansion with a turret on top.

"We climbed out and gasped at this castle. Her dad was President of Westinghouse or something. Big shot. High roller. Wheeler-dealer."

"My dad sold industrial equipment," Novak said.

"Jeff's dad was a music professor."

"My dad worked in a perfume factory," said Valenti.

"We're talking social chasm here," Rocco said.

"In we went."

Roc walked over and sat on an amplifier.

"Her mother greeted us, and shortly thereafter, Deborah joined us. On her, even a simple pleated wool plaid skirt and basic monogrammed preppy blouse looked stunning. After exchanging pleasantries, and trying not to drool on the priceless Oriental carpet, the kids were ushered upstairs.

"It was amazing how Mrs. Fenton trusted her luscious daughter in the company of three ultimate studs like us."

"Much less in her daughter's bedroom," Ron added.

"Why, any one of us could have given this girl a one-way ticket to ecstasy," Roc went on. "You'd absolutely never know we were virgins." They sang in unison:

♪

"We were. . . .            ♪

♪♪    Rock Stars to Harvard.              ♪

Not string beans to Utah.

♩    Rock Stars to Harvard! With sunglasses!"

"But she trusted us anyway," said Valenti.

Roc elaborated, "Deborah's bedroom was on the top floor of the palace, and it was about the size of my parents' living room. Like everything else in the house, it was sumptuously decorated with lavish furnishings and the finest antiques."

"We're talking ex--pen--see--vah!" Valenti interjected.

Roc went on, "Deborah showed us her collections of rare books and miniature china, and the four of us gabbed for a few hours about parents, school, philosophy and music.

"But the climax of the afternoon came with our tour of the turret." Roc stood up and walked to the front. "The turret was a small, glass-paned wooden tower about four feet high that extended skywards from the ceiling of Deborah's bedroom. It was one of the many neat features of this 18th Century mansion. Deborah pulled a smooth, lacquered ladder down from a hidden compartment in the ceiling, and climbed up it into the turret. The top of her body was in the tower, and her ankles were about even with our eye level. Standing there on the ladder, she described to us at length what a terrific view she had through the glass out onto the surrounding town and countryside.

"At that moment, *this* guy's elbow suddenly jabbed me hard in the ribs," Roc said, thrusting a thumb towards Ron. "Valenti, the Italian, noticed it first——of course. There he was, long-haired senior class valedictorian, standing there with a big shit-eating grin on his face, pointing upwards at something with his forefinger.
I looked up. Holy shit!
You could see straight up her dress!"

Ron exclaimed, "The view was perfect! No obstructions. One hundred percent visibility. It was breathtaking!"

Novak went on, "It was like being on the five yard line. You could see paydirt!
It was like looking down a pleated wool tunnel with Heaven at the other end!

"Jeff Judson was holding his sides and turning red stifling a laugh. Valenti's grin was getting wider and wider. Deborah had no idea what was going on beneath her. Her head was in the clouds. She was oblivious.
Sex was the farthest thing from her mind."
"And the closest thing to ours," Ron added.

Novak and Valenti looked at each other and laughed.

"After a minute that was savored like an hour," Valenti said, "she eventually came down, and we each took turns climbing up the ladder into the turret to look out and see the view. We pretended to be interested in the view of the surrounding countryside." He paused.
"But we'd already had *our* view."

"Low-Lifes in Paradise," said Novak, walking over to Valenti.
"True, my friends and I may have been degenerate enough to relish the view…."
"But she was dumb enough to give it to us," said Valenti.
"And that's the bottom line," said Novak.

Valenti recapped, "Deborah Fenton went on to date Heathcliff Snodgrass the Third with the Mercedes, who is now Prep Executive Yo-Yo at Eastinghouse Corporation."

"Fortunately for me," said Roc, "I went on to date Roselyn Rosenblatz with the big tits.

On to a life of grime.

Thank Goodness I went the wrong way!

Only *then* could I hit the jackpot." He paused.

"And so can you, pardy hounds," he added.

Novak stopped and looked out over the group. Barnyard animal noises and mooing sounds arose from the floor. Several orange cushions sailed through the air towards the platform. He smiled appreciatively.

A long-haired guy stood up and asked,

"Hey, Roc, if you're such a hip dude, what were you doing chasing preppies?"

Laughter circled around the room.

Roc smiled and replied, "Well, there weren't any preppie-hippies around to chase."

"Why not?" the guy asked.

"Because there is no such thing."

"How come?"

"Well," Roc said, "imagine a movie scene that goes like this....

"A young man and an older man walk out onto the driveway in front of their mansion, where a butler whisks a canvas covering off a shiny new automobile.

'Gee, Dad, Thanks!' the kid says,
**_'Nice Ferrari!'_**
And as the guy drives off in it, he says
to himself:
'I was thinking about becoming a rebel,
but now I'm wondering why.
What am I going to be?
A Rebel Against Ferraris?
No, actually, I don't think so.'

"But fortunately for you, gentle fans,
I, your humble guitar wing leader,
was not deprived like this
from the pleasures of rebelling.
And so, I went on to discover
the infinitely more cosmic dimensions
that lie beyond our normal perceptions
of life in the material world."

Novak paused for a moment and surveyed the room with
an air of wisdom.  Then he continued:

"But let's not get _fanatical_ about this.
Zealous, sure, but you have to retain 'balance.'
If we stop doing these concerts,
it'll be because some Big Money from the material world
paid us off to shut up."

A muffled guffaw arose from Valenti.  He picked up a
guitar as Novak continued speaking:

"I mean, sure, the revolution's important and everything.
But a Ferrari?
Are you kidding?
Whoa.
We're talking *serious* car here.
We're talking dream machine!

"Not that I'd ever 'sell out' or anything.
Oh, no. Not me. Not for an instant.
I'd just agree to use some *other media* for my message
that was a little more
*subtle* than this one.
Like, maybe, finger painting.
Or underwater basket weaving."

A music sting arose from Valenti's guitar.

Roc went on:
"Oh, I'd still broadcast the message, brothers and sisters,
Don't get me wrong, that wouldn't change.
It would just be in a different *art form*.
Okay?
Good.

"And, uh, could you make that a *yellow* Ferrari, please?
With ice cream on top?"

Novak grinned. Large moaning and booing noises welled
up from the group. "Thank you," he acknowledged.

One of the roadies working on the platform behind Roc walked over to him and spoke something in his ear. Roc looked at his watch.

"Time's up, everybody," he said. "It's show time. Gotta rock and roll. I'm outta here. See you in a few." And with that, he jumped up, received the applause, and left with Valenti.

The people in the room got up together, everyone talking at once, and shuffled out the doors.

"That's incredible," Kevin said to Amy as the crowd went down the stairs.
"What?" asked Amy.
"I never realized that about the Southern Hemisphere."
"You retard," giggled Amy.

# 17. **META ROCK**

The eight party hounds filed out onto the coliseum floor, where Juanita and several of her friends showed them to their seats in the V.I.P. area near the stage.

"This is exciting...." Melanie said to Brad, sitting next to her. "I've never been this close before."

"Gee," Brad replied, "I thought you had been this close a lot."

"Why?" asked Melanie.

"Well," Brad said, "the hearing difficulty, the speech impediment, the glazed look......shall I go on? Oofff!" Melanie's small fist sunk into Brad's solar plexus.

"Just kidding," Brad mumbled.

"Look at all the people," Clark said. Turning around in their seats, the eight friends saw thousands of people in the brightly-lit coliseum, some seated, some walking around. They watched the seats fill up around the sloping walls of the massive building, and then without notice, the lights went out.

A cheer erupted from the darkness, and suddenly all present were united in a bond of noise. The suspense of being in the darkness and not knowing what was happening next was all the excuse these people needed to hoot and holler to their heart's content . . . (but then, this was a rock'n'roll town).

Suddenly, a single shaft of white light exploded on center stage and bathed a human figure in brilliance. The crowd went wild.  Through the dry ice mists rising off the stage, the faint outlines of giant columns could be seen behind a raised metallic pyramid where the figure stood.  A vibrant gridwork of blue-green laser beams shot across the coliseum sky, illuminating the stage momentarily.  The columns were part of an ancient Roman temple.  From behind the mists, a voice echoed out over the crowd——

**"Before there was anything, there was The Beginning....."**

Another spotlight picked out a Sumo wrestler on stage left.  He lifted a mallet and struck a huge round golden Chinese gong that reverberated throughout the coliseum world.  **B o n n g g g !**
The cheering subsided.  Novak repeated.....

"Before there was anything, there was
The Beginning......"

"And in The Beginning, there was The Light.
On the First Day, The Light made the Earth.
And on the Second Day, The Light made Abraham.
And on the Third Day, Abraham made
the God of Forests, the God of Natural Animals,
and the God of Twinkies.

"It was magnificent!  I remember it like it was yesterday.
There I was, riding two huge golden sponge cakes across
the sky, one under each foot, like giant water skis!
That was me!"

The crowd stomped and whistled.

"Then came the Greeks. The Greeks had many gods— like Zeus, the god of Bowling; Venus, the goddess of Spandex; Mars, the god of Candy; and Athena, the goddess of Jewelry.

"Then came the Romans. The Romans also had many gods—like Neptune, the god of Drink; Saturn, the god of Amplifiers; Hera, the goddess of Aerobics, and Uranus, the god of Republicans.

"Yes, indeed.
A mighty chorus line was our Heaven.

"Then along came the Hebrews, and eventually Jesus, with the idea that Heaven was more like a corporation. This marked the transition in the Western world from p a n t h e i s m —many gods— to m o n o t h e i s m —one God. That was 2000 years ago. So here's where we are now."

A projector flashed an image onto a giant screen behind the stage.

| | | |
|---|---|---|
| PANTHEISM | MONOTHEISM | MANTHEISM |
| 2000BC | 0 | 2000    4000 |

"Today, right now, it's 2000 years later, and guess what?" Roc continued.

"We're going to have another big transition. Those of you who are *evolved* know what it is already.

"There's a big secret in the world, and it's getting ready to pop. Kind of like a zit. The Western world is built on a false premise, and that premise is about to crumble. When it does, it will be like going from pantheism to monotheism. It'll be a big improvement.

"And dirty ol' Uncle Rocco is gonna let the cat out of the bag for you right now, pardner. That's because Rocco gets a kick out of shaking things up."

"Long Live Rock'n'Roll!" yelled someone in the audience.

"The Establishment is assuming that people are solid bodies with personalities," Novak went on. "But history will show that the Establishment is a bunch of blockheads. Because *consciousness* is really where it's at, mann. People are, like, CONSCIOUSNESS UNITS. With bodies.

"The HIPPIES were the first ones to make consciousness popular. Before them, Society was nothin' but a bunch of jive-ass, fast-talkin' money-grubbing glamour-gluttons."

"Yeeee*Haw*!" hollered someone on stage.

"The Hippies weren't a bunch of lunatics.
They were RIGHT.
History will call them heros,
because they pioneered the consciousness revolution."

The crowd erupted.

"That's where the real revolution is, brothers and sisters.
Not in mere politics,
but in our very concept of life itself.

"The Aquarian Age we are entering
is when each person on Earth
awakens to his or her Divine nature
as a conscious living being.

"That's mantheism.

"So when people ask you what you believe in,
tell 'em you worship YOURSELF.

"That'll put you on a fast track to success in Hollywood, while it supercharges 'yer mind with hyperawareness.

"Mantheism. Two thousand years in the making, but it's finally here. And it's totally now. It's totally you. It's everything. It'z wuz happenin', babe. It's The New Rock'n'Roll Religion Of The Future.

"You."

Blue-green laser beams fanned out over the excited throng as the Chinese gong sounded once more.

"Now does anyone here want to see some mantheism come to life—
—right in this coliseum?"
The crowd responded.
"You do?
You sure now?"
More cheers.
"Okay, here we go. . . .
        Recently, I went to Italy to study archaeology.
        I was staying in the town near Mount Vesuvius,
        studying the ancient civilization.
        One afternoon, on the way back to my hotel,
        I stopped in an open air market.
        I bought a lot of fresh peaches
        from a man in a fruit stand.
        The man gave me something to put them in
        as I headed off for my hotel room.
Join in with me...."

A spotlight zeroed in on him and the house lights
dimmed.

> "I wedged the peaches
> in a bag
> in the untidy streets of Vesuvius.
> I opened the doorknob
> with just one hand.
>
> One station
> playing loud
> on the radio
> with caviar and custard
> for all."

Cheers rang throughout the hall.
"Pledge a legion!" Paula shouted out.
Novak received the applause with a smile, and the house
lights came on.

"Okay, people, there's 10,000 of us in here tonight.
We've got a full house.
And so we're going to have some fun.
All right?"
"All right!" they answered.

"First, I'm going to lead us through a demonstration of
group mind power.
Everybody close your eyes.
Take some deep breaths. Inhale. Hold the breath
for just a moment.
Exhale. Inhale again. Hold it for just a moment.

And exhale again.
Good.
Now concentrate on your own awareness.
And then feel the awareness of everyone else around you.
I want 10,000 minds in here all concentrating on 9,999
other minds.

"I want a group awareness. You got that?
Imagine you have twice your normal awareness.
Feel all the space around you in the coliseum.
And feel all the other minds in here too.
You're sitting in a sea of awareness.
Concentrate on that for a moment
while I am silent."

Melanie and Kevin concentrated on their awareness while
Paula glanced at the roof and noticed an oversized party
balloon fastened to the rafters. Rocco continued:

"All right. You can relax now.
Continue to *feel* the awareness all around you
as you listen to the sound of my voice.

"The New Age isn't a figment of somebody's
imagination.
The New Age rests on a power.
It's a power that scientists of the Old World don't
acknowledge.
The power of spirit.
But it's a power each of you has deep within you.
And it's a power we're going to see here tonight.

"Okay, now, people, there's a big red balloon hanging from the ceiling of this coliseum.
You probably noticed is as you came in.
Keep your eyes closed, and picture it.
And be very quiet.
Concentrate.

"Alright, now on the count of three, I want you all to imagine that red balloon
exploding in your mind.
Imagine the air inside of it becoming very hot and expanding.
*See* and *hear* the balloon popping in your mind.
Because we're about to do something wonderful here.
And I know we can do it.
Be very quiet, and listen for the pop right after I say three.
Ready?  Here we go.....
One!
Two!
THREE!"      ! ! ! ! !

"Oooooohhhhh.  Tooooo Bad.....
You *didn't* break the balloon!
Ten THOUSAND of you guys
against that *one little balloon*
and the BALLOON WINS.
How embarrassing!
Guess the *New Age* hasn't arrived **here** yet."

The great hall rocked with unrestrained hilarity.  A white
frisbee sailed out over the crowd across the coliseum.

"I'm not sure we should go on with the rest of the
program now," Novak hesitated.
"But I'll tell you what. . . .
Since I'm a nice guy, and since I like you,
I'm going to give you all a chance," he said.
"A chance to redeem your honor."

"This time, we'll try something *different*
and see how you do with *that*.
To help you along, I'll give you some
special guidance first.  Listen carefully.

"Once in a while during 7th grade, I used to sleep over at
my friend Marty Zeller's house just for fun.  His house
had a downstairs den with convertible sofas where we'd
sleep.  Eventually, that is.  But not until after we had
done a lot of wild pillow fighting.  After his mother had
hollered 'Settle Down!' at us from the kitchen a couple of
times, we would lay down our weapons and start telling
stories.

"We'd spend most of our time exchanging exaggerated, highly-animated fantasy stories about what it would be like to actually *see* and *touch* certain parts of the female anatomy. Each story would be wilder and more oversized that the last, like we were talking about something as big as hot air balloons or football stadiums.

"Marty's mother would be sitting upstairs in the kitchen, smoking cigarettes and listening to all this in disbelief, wondering whether to call a psychologist or the fire department. But before she could make up her mind, our party agenda would shift into a new phase, and the artificial farting noise contest would begin."

"Oh, boy," Amy said to Paula, rolling her eyes. "This is going to be really educational...."
"For the *guys*," Paula responded.

"To the innocent bystander, this contest sounded like gigantic ear-splitting eruptions followed by peals of high-pitched laughter. — Our voices hadn't changed yet.— This would be followed by more noises, and more laughter, and so on. Marty turned out to be the artificial farting noise contest champion. His volcanic blasts nearly shook his mom's china loose from the kitchen cabinets upstairs.

"It wasn't until recently that I learned how to make a really superior phony fart. And today is your lucky day, because I'm going to share this with you now. So pay attention, because this will be important information for some of you."

Karen looked fondly at Bruce, sitting there paying rapt attention. *Yeah, it'll be important information for you,* she thought. *You moron.*

"To make a really superior bogus blast, you have to lick your arm first. That's the secret. Then you lick your lips and place your wet forearm over your mouth and blow.
The result?
Well, if you do it right, the walls will come tumbling down.
Along with your popularity."

*You can say that again,* Paula thought.

"Now if there are any preppies in the audience tonight or people from high society, or royalty . . . .
ha ha ha ha ha ha ha yeah, *right.* . . .
you don't have to do this.
But there's no getting around the fact
that you will have to *hear* it.
So what the hell,
you might as well join in.
We promise not to tell.

"Okay, now, the crash helmets
you were issued on your way in
are in case we blow the roof off,
or bring the house down.

"So everybody, put on your crash helmets.
Put them on now. Attaboy. All 10,000 of you.
Make sure the leather strap is securely fastened under
your chin.

"To fasten the strap, insert the loose end into the metal
buckle and clasp securely. To release the buckle, lift
upward on the metal tab and remove the strap. To change
altitude, insert the strap securely between your legs and
rotate rapidly.

"Alright, now, on the count of three we're all going to
make that noise.
Remember now, I said *artificial* noises.
We issued crash helmets, not gas masks.
Okay, here we go. Everybody lick your wrists now. Get
'em good and wet. That's it. Okay, now, ready? Here
we go.

**1**    ------    **2**    ------    **3 !"**

**K K K A A A ------ B L O O M !**

---

---

"Wow, people, that was really spectacular!
I've got to write this down in my notebook.
Let's see. This is Phoenix. *Didn't*
break the balloon, but, *great* farting noise.
Phoenix. Okay. I've got your wavelength now."

Cheers and jeers floated up from the audience.

"Well, this concludes the educational portion of
our Metarock concert here tonight.
I hope you all learned something about yourselves.
I certainly learned something about you.

"And from here on, we'll be doing the
Rock 'n' Roll portion of the experience.
Is anybody up for that?"
Thunder answered him.
"Alright!!
Let's Go!!!!"

Roc leapt off the metal pyramid into a giant round bin of foam rubber. As he bounced up, somebody threw him a guitar and he lurched forward towards a microphone. Behind him, three guitar players, a drummer and a keyboard man ran on to the stage and took their positions. The band tore into a kick-ass rock'n'roll number that brought the crowd to its feet.

Paula looked over her shoulder at the people behind her. Everyone was smiling and gyrating to the sound. A musky fragrance drifted through the air. A long-haired guy in a blue t-shirt passed a pair of binoculars to her. She could practically see the pores in Roc's face. She smiled and handed the glasses back.
"We're so close up, you don't need these," she said.
"For the guitar work," he answered.

Brad watched the spotlights dance over the band and the cheering crowd. Clark, who was standing next to him, nudged him and handed him a guitar pick. Brad smiled in thanks. This was the proper way to play air guitar. You could always divide the people playing air guitar at concerts into two groups—the ones without picks and the ones who had them. *We all started as beginners*, thought Brad, *and now some of us are pros*. He tore into a liquid riff while Clark backed him up on rhythm.

Deep from within the upper reaches of the hall, a second frisbee caught the light as it floated out over the crowd. Launched by some wayward fan from high up in the far seats, the spinning disc sailed gracefully over the entire length of the coliseum.

"Impressive flight pattern," Clark said to Brad.

"Zvortyl," Brad agreed.

Karin didn't remember how long the concert lasted. She only knew she was transported to another dimension. Like all concerts, it was never long enough.

The crowd allowed the band to leave eventually, and the audience began the task of finding their way back to so-called reality. The eight friends followed Juanita through the stage exit and out to the white van in the parking lot.

## 18. <u>TAKE IT WITH YOU</u>

Amy asked Juanita to stop at a 7-11 so she could pick up a couple of them golden sponge cakes for the ride back. A few blocks later, Juanita spotted a 7-11 and pulled in. Karin and Bruce defected from the main group and went into a nearby drug store to browse. In a few minutes, the group reassembled and was on the road again.

Bruce switched on the overhead light in the roof, and pulled out a magazine from a brown paper bag. He began reading.

"Who's the centerfold this month?" Paula snickered.

"She's in the bag," Karin smirked. "This is the *other* magazine he bought along with it, to make it look good." She peered over at Bruce. "New Age.....Something," she read from the cover.

Bruce peered up from the high-brow magazine, feigned an offended look, and said, "I have a *variety* of interests, I'll have you know."

"Yeah," Karin cut in, "blondes, brunettes, redheads. . . ."

"A true Renaissance man," Paula smirked.

Bruce ignored them. "Hey, check this out," he said, and began reading.

"If you are an advanced student of metaphysics, you have gotten pretty comfy by now with the idea that you're going to be zooming through for another pass at life on Earth when you're done with this one.

"The time-honored beliefs of wise men over the last ten thousand years have hit home in you, and you know you're in for another ride. You are among the men and women on the leading edge of spiritual evolution. You're in the vanguard of the New World, and because of this, we're going to introduce you to an exciting new breakthrough in the field of soul evolution."

"Oh boy," droned Paula.
"I can't wait," said Karin, rolling her eyes.

"No," said Bruce. "Listen to this." He continued.
"If you're smart enough to get ahead *this* lifetime, and doubly smart enough to know you're coming back for *more*, then *WHY* do YOU have to start from scratch all over again like the poor slobs who don't know any better?

"Wouldn't you move ahead faster in soul evolution next lifetime if you could pick up where you left off, instead of having to spend your time building everything back up again from nothing?

"Of course you would. You could concentrate on reaching new heights instead of re-building back to where you already were before. It would be terrific.

"Not only would it be terrific......but it just might be possible! A Consortium of companies is quietly forming around an exciting new technological breakthrough that could profoundly affect our collective happiness and fulfillment during the next five hundred years.

"The product everyone is excited about is called a Computerized Aura-Print Scanner, or 'CAPS' for short. CAPS is an electronic device that can recognize auras.

"Using science to serve *spiritual* goals, researchers have applied Kirlian photography to the area of aura pattern recognition. Kirlian photography, as you may have seen at various psychic fairs and expositions, is a process which actually allows the human aura to be photographed. Its validity has been proven over and over again and is a well-documented scientific fact."

"Oh, sure," said Amy. "I go to psychic expositions all the time."
"Me too," chimed in Karin. "We get our nails done."

Bruce was undaunted. "By blending Kirlian photography with computerized pattern recognition," he continued, "researchers were able to develop the CAPS device. This remarkable apparatus can actually scan and identify patterns in the human aura much like a voiceprint. CAPS has shown that the energy patterns in the human aura are almost as unique as voiceprints or fingerprints from one individual to the next.

"This breakthrough opens up an entirely new dimension in the area of 'soul identification,' and in fact, we have an emerging science capable of correctly identifying individuals by their auric energy patterns."
He paused to turn the page in the magazine.

"We can already identify you through your warped mind patterns, Bruce," said Clark.

"And when you IQ rises to 38, sell," advised Brad.

Bruce laughed and resumed reading:

"Since the soul travels intact from one lifetime to the next, this new technology has staggering implications for trans-lifetime soul identification. A Kirrillian aura-print taken in one lifetime could be matched up to identify the person in their next lifetime!

"A number of companies are taking this new technology very seriously. If it can be completely perfected, it means nothing short of a direct assault on the age-old adage of 'You can't take it with you.' The benefits for everyone involved could be nothing short of fantastic!"

"Wow!" exclaimed Melanie. "How do we do it?"

"To take advantage of this emerging new technology," Bruce continued reading, "a Consortium of companies has started the world's first Trans-Incarnation Investment Fund. This Fund provides a tax-sheltered investment vehicle which allows you to place your assets, deeds, titles, and personal belongings into a special safe deposit box."

"Just what I need," moaned Paula. "A tax shelter."

"Is this for preppies, or what?" said Melanie.

Bruce forged on. "The safe deposit box is electronically activated by recognition of your aura's energy pattern. Valuables that you place on deposit will be held in trust by the Consortium for eventual release back to you in your next lifetime. For this service, the Consortium charges a modest fee amounting to half the interest accruing on the value of the deposited items on an annual basis.

"To reclaim your stocks, bonds, deeds and other valuables when you incarnate into your next lifetime, you merely go to one of the Consortium's local offices and submit yourself for electronic CAPS scanning of your aura. When your aura pattern is correctly recognized, the box opens, and all the valuables that you've stashed away from your previous lifetime will be yours!"

"Wow!" exclaimed Brad.
"A timeless stash!" squealed Melanie.

"Now, we appreciate that the Age of Aquarius is dawning," Bruce continued, "but we also realize that it hasn't dawned everywhere yet, and we still live in an imperfect world. Unfortunately, there are bound to be certain unscrupulous individuals who invariably will try to 'break the system' and get into other people's accounts, particularly if the funds involved are very large, which in some cases, they will be."

Juanita interrupted Bruce and told everyone to look out the back window. The city lights sparkled beautifully in the distance behind them as the van climbed into the desert hills.

Bruce resumed, "To ensure your complete protection against unauthorized access to your account by impersonators, the Consortium provides a *double security guarantee* feature. In addition to electronically recording your aura's unique energy patterns when you deposit your valuables, you will also be given a special trans-incarnation security debriefing. The security debriefing will contain an exchange of confidential information known only to you and to a bonded officer of the Consortium. This special information forms the 'second ring' of protection between your account and unauthorized individuals attempting to access it."

"So impersonators can't get in?" Kevin asked Paula.
"Yeah, I think so," she replied.

Bruce went on, "To reclaim your funds and other valuables in your next lifetime, you first report to your local Consortium office for electronic scanning of your aura. After the computer recognizes your aura-print, you then repeat the confidential information to gain final access to your account.

"The specific confidential information for you to remember in your next lifetime will be assigned to you by the Consortium. Typically, it will consist of an easy-to-remember code number, like 070-3529-18527-807-24806-1109, along with something noteworthy to you, such as your ex-mother-in-law's deodorant preference. (Unclaimed funds remain the property of the Consortium.)"

Bruce's audience erupted in an uproar.

He concluded reading:

"For more information on these fabulous Zvortyl Incarnation Trust Services, write to me, Johnny Rockit, c/o ZITS, 119 N. El Camino Real, Suite 200, Encinitas, California 92024. Let us show *you* how you *can* take it with you——with Zvortyl!"

Karin grabbed the magazine out of Bruce's hands and flung it towards the back seat. Barnyard animal noises filled the air.

When the din subsided, Bruce looked up to the front seat at the driver. "Juanita," he said, "do you agree with the article?"

"Sure, baby," the driver answered. "How do you think we bought this van?"

# 19. *Mindsurfing*

Early the next day, Tara called her class to order. She was excited about teaching Mindsurfing to this new group. "Before we begin," she said, "let me ask you all a question. What's the most exciting thing you can think of that you'd like to learn about today?"

Tara paused and smiled. In her mind, the class answered: "Mindsurfing!" in a unanimous cheer.

"Tugboat Design," replied Amy.
"Diversified Theories of Bowling," said Bruce.
"Napkin Folding," volunteered Karin.
"Air Guitar Acrobatics," answered Clark.
"Leaf Pressing," said Amy.

*Just what I need*, thought Tara——*a bunch of smartass tenderfoots.*

"Economics of Macramé," suggested Paula.
"Trigonometry of Golf," answered Kevin.
"Principles of Spanking," ventured Melanie.
"Harp Psychology," quipped Karin.
"Stain Removal Analysis," responded Amy.
"Religious Studies of Poster Art," said Brad.
"Adrenal Technologies," replied Kevin.
"Slalom Sciences," offered Clark.
"Happy Face Engineering," said Melanie.

"Fine," Tara huffed. "Be that way. But she who laughs last laughs best."

With that, she doused the lights and turned on a television monitor in front of the room. A man in a toga holding a huge javelin appeared in front of a temple that looked like Mount Olympus. He spoke nobly:

> "Mind. Wind.
> Wind. Mind.
> Nowhere. Now Here.
> Hear now these silent words of
> imprisoned ecstasy....
> Like a stricken god, I hurl my curse
> of echoing laughter at the winds of words!"

"Oooops," Tara interrupted. "Sorry. Wrong channel." She flicked a control, and a tall man in a yellow duck suit came on, flapping his wings and quacking:

> "HI 'ya BOYS 'n' GIRLS!
> We've got LOTS-a FUN to COME your WAY—
> So let's all yell HIP-HIP-HOORAY!
> For the JOHnny GOO-roo SHOW to-DAY!
> YAAAYY!"

"There," sneered Tara, "is that better for you.......
children?" She flashed a victory smile. "Yes?" she asked. "Good."

The program continued: "The foist thing on our show today is twavel," the duck said. "Here's a tawiffic twavel tip for a twip without tripe. Next time yaw in Hawaii, dwop by the north shore of Oahu, and check out Sunset Beach or Wiamea Bay. Tweet yawself to the unfawgettable sights and sounds of macho lunatics surfing on twenty foot high steamrollers. On a Big Day, dare can be fifty or maw surfanatics out dare at Sunset Beach. Tawk about thrill-seeking. Whoa! Quack, quack, quack!"

The screen went blank momentarily, and Kevin and Amy stared at each other briefly, in disbelief. Then the oversized duck reappeared on a white sandy beach, holding a microphone, talking to Roc and Rusty. "What is it wit you guys and surfing?" quacked the duck.

"Surfing is exhilarating because it feels like you can fly," answered Roc. "You're like Superman. You're slicing through space without touching the Earth, and there's no ski poles or tow ropes. It's like you're flying through fluid on your own. It's a gas!
Wheeeeee!
There you have it —— the essence of surfing.
Wheeeeee!
Like four year olds.
Have I got your wave length now?"
He paused, and looked at the duck.
"I thought so," he said.
A gust of wind blew into the microphone.

"Joe Surf and Surfer Girl don't usually debate the quark theory of atomic physics," Rusty added.
"They're into Wheeeeee! . . . . .
On and off the beach."

"And you don't find that many heavy intellectuals or research scientists out there on surfboards," said Roc.
"Because Wheeeeee! is too simple for them.
But gas what.
You won't find them dancing with the angels either.
Because Wheeeeee! is what Kolinar is all about."
He paused.
"And you're about to get a peak at it now."

The image disappeared and Tara turned the lights on.
The group was nonplused.
Nobody spoke.    Finally, Paula asked, "What does Mindsurfing have to do with ducks?"
"Quack, quack, quack!" replied Tara.
This broke the ice.  Everyone relaxed.
"So what is Mindsurfing?" Bruce asked.
"You get to Kolinar by Mindsurfing," Tara answered.
"Mindsurfing is a dramatic new breakthrough in human awareness which allows you, the party animal, to blast off into orbital altitudes you've never dreamed of before. . . .
There are no creams, no messy ointments, no mechanical apparatus of any kind. . . . .
Everything is done for you!
Experience thrill upon thrill as you hurtle headlong upward past levels of levity you never imagined before!"

Brad appeared suspicious.

"Don't worry," whispered Melanie, "she's a quack."

Brad looked relieved.

"How does Mindsurfing work?" asked Paula.

"You, the party animal, ride on a Mindsurfing surfboard called a *rockstar*," Tara answered. "The rockstar floats you and propels you over your mental ocean of wayward humanoid thoughtforms." She flipped on an overhead projector and a drawing appeared.

"The rockstar is a certain rock'n'roll energy thought pattern that you impress upon your mind," Tara continued. "It has the effect of elevating you above ordinary thinking. The rockstar invokes the unchained cosmic power of rock'n'roll, which causes you to experience a mental buoyancy.

"You ride the rockstar on brainwaves. Little brainwaves at first, then later, when you develop more skill, larger brainwaves that lift you higher off the surface of the water.

"Occasionally, you will wipe out and fall off your rockstar. You will be submerged back into your ocean of wayward humanoid thoughtforms. When you surface once again, you climb back on board your rockstar and paddle out for another wave."

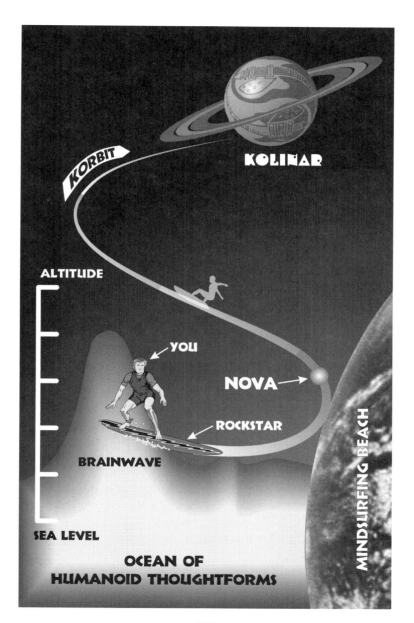

KORBIT

KOLINAR

ALTITUDE

YOU

NOVA

ROCKSTAR

BRAINWAVE

MINDSURFING BEACH

SEA LEVEL

OCEAN OF
HUMANOID THOUGHTFORMS

"Better have a motorized rockstar for Paula," Brad chuckled.

"Better have a scuba dive suit for Brad," Paula countered.

"Alright you two," Tara said, unable to suppress a smile.

"Now as you progress further and gain proficiency," she continued, "you are able to handle larger and larger brainwaves successfully. When you finally obtain Kolinar Clearance, you will be granted admission to the Big Time. Your Kolinar Clearance is your ticket to the Bonzai Wiamea Bay Pipeline. When you ride one of *these* suckers, and do it the right way, it will catapult you right out of the water. At this point, called *Nova*, you achieve liftoff, and you are on your way to reaching korbital velocity."

"How do I hit the jackpot?" Clark asked.

Tara walked over to the projector and pushed a button. Another image appeared.

"As you see here," she explained, "your liftoff takes you up through the stratosphere into k-orbit——an orbit from which you can touch Kolinar. During korbit, you will be following the confidential and unbelievably powerful procedures contained in the Kolinar Clearance pack.

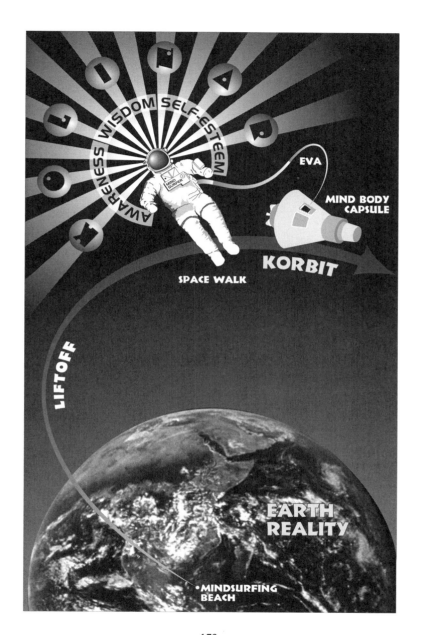

"These incredible new discoveries will lift your astonished butt right out of your body-mind capsule, and onto a space walk in the galaxy.[1] Weightless, surrounded by space, tethered to your capsule, and staring the universe in the face, you then cross the threshold into the incomparable experience of KOLINAR."

Tara finished.
"Wow…….." echoed Clark and Kevin in unison.
Tara looked over her class. "Are there any questions?" she asked.
"Yes," replied Amy. "When do we learn about Napkin Folding?"

---

[1] Extra Vehicular Activity (EVA)

# 20.  TALK SHOW

It looked more like an underground library than a lunch room, with overhead monitors and bookshelves lining the rock walls, but this was the place Karin had chosen to surprise Bruce on his birthday.  A cluster of friends had gathered to watch Bruce blow out the candles on his cake, and share in the proceeds.

After the cake was cut and the festivities were underway, Karin found herself sitting in between Bruce and Clark. She noticed that Clark was staring at her with a very large piece of birthday cake in his mouth.  His eyes were crossed and his mouth was wide open.  Worse, he was probably doing it deliberately (although with Clark one could never be sure).

"Believe it or not, Clark," Karin said to him, "your horizons really do extend further than going to laundromats for the rest of your life.  True, you may not have proper breeding.  But you can fake it.  Let me show you how."
Clark vaguely paid attention.

"First, there's nothing worse than sitting at the dinner table and seeing somebody else's open mouth, full of food," she lectured.
"I really don't want to know
the contents of your inner mouth
especially when it's full of food.
Keep it to yourself, spaz.

"And I also don't want to hear
all the crunchy smacking noises
your food makes when you mash on it with your teeth.
Other people's food
when it's in their mouths
is totally disgusting.
Especially yours.

"So close your mouth when you chew, wasteoid."

Clark obliged.   You could only mess with Karin up to a
certain point.   After that, it was dangerous.

"Now you may realize that this makes it impossible
to talk and eat at the same time," Karin continued.
"Bravo!
Brilliant deduction.

"However, if you are mentally deficient to begin with
— and we know you are —
then you will make a better impression
if you do not say anything at all.
Just sit there, bozo,
and stuff your face
and try to look good
and appear intelligent.
Fake it.
And if you're a good actor
and you don't betray yourself by opening your mouth,
mumbling, picking your teeth, or hiccuping,
you might be able to fool someone you want to impress."

Amy and Melanie giggled. Karin concluded:
"Your impeccable table manners
will create an aura of distinction
which surrounds you
kind of like a halo.

"People will think you're a high-roller
who's laundering T-Bills through Switzerland
instead of tumbling t-shirts through Laundry Land.

"And your friends will be amazed
at the change that's come over you.
A new you —
Headed for the high life now!"

Cheers and laughter reverberated in the room. Clark smiled a handsome grin. Getting slam-dunked by Karin was one of his favorite pastimes at parties. He glanced over his shoulder and saw Derek come in.
"Hey, Derek," he said, "join the party."
"Sure thing," Derek said, and conveyed congratulations to Bruce.
Karin cut a slice of cake for Derek, which he enthusiastically accepted.
"By the way," Derek mentioned, "something interesting is going on topside."
"What is it?" Karin asked.
Derek reached over and turned on one of the monitors.
"We're getting more publicity," he told her.

The monitor came on, and Rocco was just sitting down with a talk show host. As the applause subsided, the host opened it up:

"Okay, so twenty years ago, nobody believed in UFOs and now everybody does. UFOs are chic, they're totally in. Now that's progress."

"That's right, Bob," replied Roc. Turning to the television audience, he asked:

"As a matter of fact, what were *You* doing before you tuned in?" He stopped and listened.

"What's that? Okay. You say you just finished your dinner of Kazoos au Gratin and doggie yum-yums, and you and your Main Squeeze were watching 'Sex Kittens From Zorbitron' on Channel 10. It was a blast. Little stars and planets were flashing and blinking at you. Ummmmm. See? That proves it. An intergalactic transmission. Quick, recite the multiplication tables!"

He paused.

"Now, what does this mean?" he continued.

"Yes, what *does* this mean?" Bob prompted.

"Well, the universe is a big place," Roc explained, "so if there's life buzzing around out there in flying saucers in *this* galaxy, why not in *other* galaxies? It's not like the Milky Way is white and everything else is purple. The Milky Way isn't God's greatest galaxy; it's not the Israel of the Universe, it's just another star cluster. So what goes on here can happen practically anywhere.

## A Special Note To Reviewers of the Prototype Edition

This book is written for a lower IQ bracket audience than your esteemed self.

Therefore, it contains references, especially in the beginning, to sex, drugs, rock'n'roll, women in tight-fitting clothing, overindulgence, and, worst of all, flatulence.

Weaving these low-IQ subjects into the book is a *literary device* for galvanizing the attention of my target audience, many of whom are young and male.
And stupid.

The result is a sleazy philosophy book which hits a new low for metaphysics, but has mass appeal.

If you are a person of refinement and distinction, then you may be offended by certain passages in the book, and in fact, you may not want to read it.

If this happens to you, just remind yourself that you are not a member of the book's target audience, thank God, and try to appreciate the work for its literary value (if any).

Conversely, if you manage to get through all this mindless mayhem without ever feeling offended---in fact, actually *liking* it, then put your hands on the radio, yell Hallelujah, Brother, and join the Rock'n'Roll State of Mind!

"Now, I know trying to imagine sentient life whizzing around almost every galaxy would overload your feeble mind, so I'm going to make it easy for you. All you have to do is imagine there is life on a thousand other planets. You can handle that. You passed algebra, didn't you? Well, that was harder than this."

"If you didn't pass algebra," Bob interjected, "or if you can't count as high as a thousand, go back to Channel 10. You'll be fine."

The audience chuckled. In the control room, Bob's producer gleamed, thinking, *Attaboy, Bob, stick it to Channel 10!*

On a roll, Bob continued. "Okay, so people are on a thousand planets," he said. "Big deal. If you're, like, an avant-garde cosmic consciousness advocate, you're probably thinking that's conservative."

"You're right, Bob, I am," Roc replied. "But it doesn't matter what the *number* is. The *point* is, all our senators, ambassadors, diplocrats, and heads of slate want *you* to think that UFOs are *bunk*.

And that's hype. Or tripe. One of those."

Brad looked around for a dictionary. Tripe? What the hell was tripe?

"Yeah, go ahead and look it up, dork," Roc said.

"**I** had to.

I get my rhyme, and you get a trip to the dictionary.

And worse, you paid for it."

Brad was dumbfounded. "Me?" he said. "Is he talking to me?"

Behind him, Karin snickered.

"There you go....." Roc resumed.
"All expenses paid.
Bon Voyage.
It's under 'T'.
Send a postcard.
Adios.
Dork.

"Don't think *I'm* going to define it for you.
What do you want—
a running translation for the mentally-impaired?
No such luck, bozo.
Yeah, sure, I think society is bullshit.
But I'll have you know **I** dropped out of
an *Ivy League* school.
And you didn't even get into one.
Not if you don't know what 'tripe' means.
Because they have a lot of things at Ivy League
universities.
And tripe is one of them.

"So this is aerobics.
You've got dictionary destiny.
You're dictionary-bound, buddy.
There's a dictionary in your very near future.
So get off your butt and go get a dictionary.

And then do fifty leg lifts.
Couch potato.
Dork."

Roc seemed finished for the moment.
"Were you talking to someone in particular," asked Bob, "or just raving?"
"I was talking to several people in your television audience, Bob," Roc replied. "They know who they are."
"You're not serious, of course."
"I am serious, Bob."
Bob said to the camera, "Our guest has been Roc Novak."
Roc laughed. "Okay, you win," he said.
Bob relaxed.

Back on the Base, new faces began filtering into the lunch room.
"Come on in," Derek motioned to a bunch of people gathered around the doorway. "We're getting more publicity."
"How's it going?" asked Melanie.
"Bonzai, Melanie," Derek answered.

"For those of you who just joined us," Bob said, "we're talking to Roc Novak of the Zvortyl Party." He turned to Roc, saying, "I understand you have one of your key people here with you who can tell us more about the Zvortyl Party."
"Yes, we do," said Roc.
"Please welcome Diana Yagoda," Bob told his audience.

Both men rose to greet Diana as she walked on stage in a black evening gown.

Diana sat down on Roc's right, her poise and grace evident in her posture and her opening conversation with her host. After the initial chit-chat, Bob threw her a curve ball.

"Your detractors claim that your Party is chock full of hedonists," he said to Diana.

"That's true, Bob," she replied, "we are."

Bob's eyebrows went up. Roc grinned.

"But," she went on, "we also promote the personal empowerment of our members."

"At a price, of course," countered Bob.

"Why sure," Diana said. "This is America."

"Your critics claim your fees are exorbitant," Bob went on, "and that you're only in it for the money."

"That's not true," replied Diana. "And in fact, I've prepared a film segment to address that concern."

Bob looked into his studio audience and asked, "Does that interest anybody?"

The crowd came to life. "Okay," he said.

"Jerry?" he called to stage left, "Can we roll the film clip?" Jerry signaled back.

"Okay," said Bob. "On the monitor."

The spot rolled. An actor in a pinstripe suit walked onto a stage containing a waist-high plexiglass cylinder pedestal, backlit by dramatic blue and purple lighting. A miniature detailed replica of a pyramid, about two feet high, sat atop the pedestal.

"I *should* be able to walk through walls by now," the actor said, "but my outlook on life isn't quite rich enough yet."

The camera moved in closer.

"Do you feel this way, too?"

He paused, placing his hand on the pyramid. "....Yes??"

"Then you have not achieved the true Egyptian UFO Crystal Prosperity Consciousness. *So solly.*"

Bob's eyes widened. The actor went on:

"You see, with this Egyptian Prosperity Consciousness, thirty or forty thousand dollars will seem like loose change or pocket money to you. And that helps to put the forty thousand you spend for it into a more proper perspective. A mere drop in the ocean of abundance.

"Our four-dimensional, advanced-technology Egyptian UFO Crystal Prosperity Course is normally priced at $31,765. But RIGHT NOW, for a limited time only, and for you only, we are having a one-time special introductory offer, where you can have the WHOLE Egyptian UFO Crystal Prosperity Course—8 tapes in all— for only $899.95!"

The camera came in closer.

"When YOU achieve *The Zvortyl Effect* through our high-speed, laundromatic vegetation crystals, your life will s k y r o c k e t in abundance! This advanced formula cleans your mind like a Washday Miracle——and costs only pennies a day.

"So act now. Call 1-800-ZVORTYL and reserve your prosperity course today.
Credit cards accepted. 'Vene, Vidi, Visa.'
Cah-Jing, Cah-Jing, Cah-Jing, Cah-Jing, Cah-Jing.
Ho, ho, ho, ho, ho, ho, ho, ho."

The monitor went out and Bob was back on camera. He looked impressed.
"How about that...." he thought aloud, "....so it *is* reasonably priced."
"Incredible discounts," Diana said confidently, brushing her hair back.
"Eight tapes in all," echoed Roc.
"Well, you learn something every day," admitted Bob.
"Maybe you guys aren't low-lifes after all," he snickered.
"Not only that," Roc affirmed, "but we dedicate a lot of our time to the finer things in life, like arts and culture."
"And, we care about social issues," Diana added.
"No kidding," said Bob, evidently moved by the film clip.
*My God*, thought Diana, *I can't believe he bought it.*
"And here to join us tonight," continued Roc, "is one of our resident artists, Rusty Seawood, with a special poetry reading." He faced Bob. "With your permission?"
"Sure," Bob told him.

A spotlight zeroed in on a podium on stage left, and from behind the curtains, Rusty emerged and took the rostrum. "This poem is entitled *Tubular Sorority*," he began.

"If people are yuppies
They don't have puppies.
Ever notice that?
Or if they do,
It's one or two,
Never any more.

"Raising children?
What a hassle.
Little monsters
Trash your life.

"Having children?
What women go through?
Shitting a watermelon?
I don't think so.

"It's grotesque.
It's like Halloween.
Chainsaw haircut?
Drano enema?
Shit a watermelon?
There's no way.

"Gross! Barf out!

"Enough already.

"Where are the test tube babies?
Bring on the Men of Science.
The Dinks.

"A dink is a dork
Without the cork.
So have a drink,
Dink."

"I think some of you foxy ladies ought to form a National Sorority with a hot priority," Rusty ad libbed. "First, you ought to drag some of your sister dinks out of nuclear physics and get them to apply their wits to this problem. Next, you ought to find out who are the guy dinks that are working on the test tube babies, track them down, and start fucking the living daylights out of them.
Make it notorious.
Make it a college dude's number one career choice.
Get smart.
Don't rely on *The Government* to solve this for you.
Do you really think they care?
Take matters into your own hands!
Lord knows you have the power.
Use it, for Christ's sake.

"Hit it with all you got, sisters,
with your bodies, hearts and minds.
'Cause it's your problem. Not mine. I mean yeah, sure, it's my problem too, intellectually. And I empathize with you. But **I** don't have to face that bullshit.
**You** do.

So git down!  Get funky!  And blow it away."
Rusty stepped down from the podium with a grin.

Bob's face wore a shell-shocked expression.  Maybe inviting these lunatics on the show wasn't such a hot idea after all.

The eruption of female enthusiasm from the audience caught Bob by surprise.  A wild cheer arose, and women started throwing things and running towards the stage.  A pair of hot pink panties landed in front of Bob.  His veteran reflexes kicked in.
"We'll be right back after this word from our sponsor," he said with a forced smile, and the studio mayhem faded into an oil portrait of a large, matronly woman standing in a country kitchen.

A professional voice behind the portrait announced:
"Tonight, Bob is being brought to you by. . . . . . . .
Fletcher's Baking Powder."
"What?" Karin squawked.
"Mother Fletcher knew what was good," the voice continued, "and she put all of that good shit into Mother Fletcher's Baking Powder . . . . .
—a little herb, a little calcium nitrate, a little magic dust...."
The portrait smiled.

"Not many people bake today, especially you young women, but sales of Fletcher's continue strong.  You see, Fletcher's is *more* than just a baking powder—it's kind of a general home remedy.  Use it for a salad seasoning, a topping for your breakfast cereal, or as a mild laundry detergent."

Brain cells on overload, Derek flipped the channel.

"Good morning, photo students," a man in a white lab coat said.  "Welcome to *TWIG—A—MODEL—TREE— the Fat-Free Formula For Fashion Philosophy.*  As you know by now, the camera adds ten pounds to your subject's appearance, so you, the photographer, have to compensate.  For instance, who can tell me what kind of model we would choose for a tree?"

*What the hell is this?* Amy said to herself.

"Yes, Salvatore?  That's right.  A twig.
So, has everyone got an anorexic model ready?
Okay, let's go.

"First, take the meridian angle of the *jaw line*, and multiply it by the hypotenuse of the *ear lobe*.  Align this to the radian of the camera angle.  Take the vector of the emitted *light beam*, and divide by the circumference of the *hemline*.  If the quotient is greater than zero, use a blow dryer.

"Now, carefully measure the diameter of the major curvatures.  Arrange your studio lighting to amplify the positive dimensions.

"Next, check the light meter, and inflate any tight or restrictive clothing. Project the full-blown image onto a lighted transparency, using a styrofoam rectifier, and adjust the swivel.
Breathe normally.

"Focus the aperture on the curvature, being careful to avoid divestiture.
Let set for thirty minutes. Model should be gold now and ready to chute."

Derek turned it off. "Enough of that," he grunted. "Let's continue with the real thing." He turned to Clark.
"Clark," Derek said, "did you know that your horizons really do extend further than going to laundromats for the rest of your life?"
"Yes," Clark replied, "we've covered that."
"Well good," Derek said, "because you'll need that insight to handle the Mindsurfing session tomorrow. Tara will pick you all up around ten."

## 21. BEGINNING MINDSURFING

The next morning, Tara and two husky boys with backpacks arrived at the group's quarters. One boy handed out small black computers to everybody, and the other one gave each person a sleek green metallic box and a canvas carrying case.

Thus equipped, the eight friends disembarked with Tara through subterranean catacombs which led into a dimly-lit red rock tunnel. Faraway music sounded in the distance ahead of them. As Paula and her companions advanced, they came to a side opening wider than any of the others Paula had seen. Paula slowed her pace, staring at a room crowded with children sitting cross-legged on a maroon-carpeted floor. At a white board against the far wall stood a woman in a yellow wraparound.

The party animals pushed forward, passing knots of people, and the tunnel bent to the right. Tara slowed and turned around, facing her crew. "We're coming to a marker," she told them. "You should have a look at this."

They came up to a large, rectangular silver plate fused into the red rock wall. It was inscribed:

# JOHNNY ROCKIT's REPORT CARD

## COURSE : HUMAN LIFE

| SUBJECT | A | B | C | D | F |
|---|---|---|---|---|---|
| | GRADE | | | | |
| COLLEGE | | INCOMPLETE | | | |
| ELECTRIC GUITAR | | B+ | | | |
| BLONDES | A+ | | | | |
| PARTYING | A | | | | |
| WATER SKIING | | | C+ | | |
| SUNGLASSES | | B+ | | | |
| COOL DANCER | A- | | | | |
| SEX | A+ | | | | |
| ROCK'N'ROLL | A+ | | | | |
| SURFING | | B- | | | |
| SHOT PUT | | | | | F |
| BASKETBALL | | | | D- | |
| FAMILY | | | | D | |
| HOLIDAY SPIRIT | | | | D+ | |
| CHURCHGOING | | | | | F |
| TABLE MANNERS | | | C+ | | |
| SNORKELING | | B- | | | |
| SAILING | | | C- | | |
| SUNBATHING | | B+ | | | |
| ROCK CONCERTS | A+ | | | | |
| BUSINESS | | B | | | |
| PROCREATION | | | | | F |
| RECREATION | A | | | | |
| HYPERAWARENESS | A+ | | | | |

Paula poked the plaque with her forefinger.
"You look at this," she sneered, "and you say to yourself:
'This guy's a real loser.
He gets flying colors in life's vices,
and only a **B** in business.'"

Brad put his thumbs behind imaginary suspenders, and
with his best good 'ol boy voice, twanged:
"Luke, this goofball is a lower form of life.
Let's round him up and get him the hell outta here,
before he pollutes the minds of us all."

Karin joined the fray. "Mothers, don't let your sons grow
up to be like this," she warned. "Take them to Idaho.
That will help."

"And girls," Amy added, "none of you in your right
minds would ever go out on a *date* with a flake like this."

"At least, none of you *nice* girls would," Melanie chirped.
"As for the rest? Well......heh, heh, heh....."

"All right, class," cut in Tara, "that's enough.
Let's move along so we stay on time."

The students forged ahead down the rock passageway and
within minutes reached the Mindsurfing Area. Derek was
adjusting a projector in front of the room. They all sat
down on thick cushions. Tara stayed with them.

Derek welcomed everyone and gave each person a short blue cable. "The blue cable connects your green box to your black computer," Tara explained to Bruce and Amy.

"The first thing you do to begin Mindsurfing," Derek said, "is to build your own personal *rockstar*. The rockstar is a collection of word-sounds from rock'n'roll. These word-sounds are arranged in a visual pattern. The pattern is in the shape of a surfboard. This shape is very important, because it allows you to ride brainwaves." He plugged a green box into Brad's computer, and went on:

"You are about to learn a potent new Third Millennium interdimensional awareness amplifying maneuver. It uses the word-sounds in your rockstar. To begin with, you will build your own personal rockstar on the computers you got this morning using the Mindsurfing program. This program allows your computer to display your rockstar for you whenever you go Mindsurfing."

Tara removed a set of Mindsurfing program disks from a compartment in the back of the room and handed one to each person.

Derek went on, "The fun begins when you start to see your rockstar change shape and color at the same time you experience mental changes yourself during Mindsurfing. This is really cool. You will be amazed to see the rockstar display change colors before your eyes in response to changes in your own internal state. It's like watching your mind on TV!"

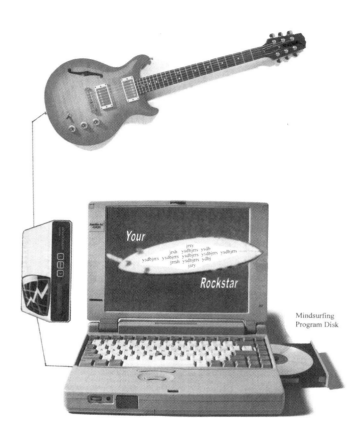

Your

Rockstar

Mindsurfing
Program Disk

"How does it work?" asked Brad.

Derek projected an image on the wall and replied, "As you can see here, Brad, all you do is plug your electric guitar into your personal computer, and hold it while you mindsurf. The magic green box you got earlier today does the rest."

"What if we don't have a guitar?" Melanie asked.

"Borrow a friend's," answered Derek.

Melanie hesitated.

"If you don't *know* anybody who owns an electric guitar," Tara commented, "perhaps joining the boy scouts or girl scouts would be more your speed."

Derek jumped right in. "You know Aunt Marge needs help this year with the hog display at the fair," he said. "Why don't you go help her out? Okay?"

"And don't forget some of your Aunt Bertha's rhubarb pie," Tara added. "Mmm, Mmmm! Now *there's* a good time."

"You lost me," Melanie said.

"Just kidding," Derek admitted. "Here's your guitar." He reached into a wall closet and started passing out electric guitars.

"Before you can go Mindsurfing, you need a beach," said Tara, while Derek handed out the instruments. "So, you will need to pick out a spot to use for Mindsurfing. If you are a high-roller, you can appropriate one of the rooms in your four-story mansion as your Mindsurfing beach. Or, if you are a low-life like us, you can pick a spot somewhere in your apartment, or, if you're on the Base, your living quarters. It doesn't matter whether you designate a room or a spot. Either method is equally effective, as long as you have control over the immediate environment.

"Next, you'll need to take steps to ensure that telephones, pets, outside noises, dinosaurs, and other people do not intrude on your beach while you are Mindsurfing. Otherwise, you'll miss the waves."

"When are you supposed to mindsurf?" Bruce asked, getting the feel of the guitar.

"Most rockers either mindsurf in the morning, before beginning the day's activities, or in the evening, after finishing them," Derek replied. "This is because it's the easiest to get into Mindsurfing when you are not moving at high speed or involved with a lot of other activities. So try it at the beginning or the end of the day."

"How long do you mindsurf?" Amy questioned him.

"You should go Mindsurfing once a day for 15 minutes," Derek answered. "If you happen to exceed this time limit, it's okay. But you should put a clock somewhere in view from your beach so you know what time it is. Remember, 15 minutes is only one percent of your day."

"How do we know when we're ready for takeoff?" asked Clark, plugging his guitar into the green box.

Derek answered, "At the completion of the Mindsurfing Course, you will return your Mindsurfing program disk and magic box to your Kahuna, which will probably be me or Tara." He flicked on an oscilloscope mounted in the wall. The green screen came to life. He went on, "There is no graduation 'test.' Your Kahuna simply plugs your magic box into an analyzer, like this, and looks at the recordings of your Mindsurfing sessions that are logged inside it. If you have achieved the required degree of brainwave mastery, as measured by the recordings of your sessions, you pass. You Kahuna will give you the final okay for Kolinar Clearance."

Tara added, "If your instructor is in a particularly good mood, he or she may be willing to overlook an occasional missed or goofy session on your part." She raised an eyebrow. "But we recommend that you don't push your luck."

"Face it," said Derek. "This isn't like lifting barbells. This isn't like training for a triathlon. This is a creampuff."

"If you can't muster the mental acuity to do *this* little flashdance," Tara said, "and by some miracle you shmooze your way past our inspectors and out on to the runway, the Lions will be waiting for you at the Gates, and your flight will be diverted to La-La Land, your home territory, we are sure."

\* \* \*

# 22. **UNITED STATES OF BEING**

Melanie wandered happily down an unfamiliar passageway, reveling in her newfound freedom. When she achieved Nova a few days earlier, she had been awarded unrestricted access to any area in the Base. Now she was taking advantage of it.

As she advanced down the corridor, she reached an open archway leading into what looked like an office of some kind. Impulsively, Melanie strode through the opening and found a young bearded man at work behind a desk. His desk was a plexiglass slab supported on either end by metallic cubes. On the wall behind him was a large photograph of the Capitol Building in Washington, D.C.

"What *is* this?" Melanie asked blankly.
"Oh, hi there," replied the young man. "This is the U.S.O.B. Office. I'm Marlin."
"Melanie," she replied. "Zvortyl." She looked at him. "What the heck is the U.S.O.B.?"
"Zvortyl," he answered. "The United States of Being — U.S.O.B.— is the Alternative Government that interfaces to the U.S. of A. It is made up of senators and representatives from the major states of being."
"Oh, really," said Melanie flatly. By now, nothing surprised her. "How does it work?"
Marlin gestured, "The U.S.O.B. meetings are conducted via HIGH Tech NOL o-gee VID-eo TEL--a--CON--ferencing HEY!"

Melanie wondered, *does he think I'm some goofball who doesn't know what video teleconferencing is?*

"So in our case," Marlin continued, "each U.S.O.B. senator has the video teleconferencing equipment installed in their office or home, and participates in weekly video telecongresses. Subcommittee meetings are also held via video. It's like, Video Government, man. Hey! Why not? We have Video Everything Else.

"A live session of congress convenes one weekend per month. Lucky members fly in Friday night and leave Sunday evening. The other members take a mule team and have to stay all week. The home of the congress is located in a secret vibratory place known only to Johnny Rockit and the Inner Pocket," Marlin concluded.

This guy was hard to swallow, but Melanie stayed with it. She pointed to the picture behind him and asked, "Why do you have the Capitol on the wall?"

"The U.S.O.B. has a lobby office in Washington, D.C. patterned after the lobbyists employed by General Motors, I.E. DuPont, Exxon, U.S. Steel, and so on," Marlin explained. "The lobbyists use their time-tested professional skills—money, name-calling, cash, sex, blackmail, scandal; the usual—to influence the U.S. Government according to the resolutions of the U.S.O.B. congress."

Marlin reached behind him and pulled a green sheet of paper out of a file drawer.

"But what do you stand for?" Melanie questioned him.

"Our campaign rhetoric runs something like this..." he replied.

"'Now that we have converged on the Third Millennium, it is time for the Hippies to start driving the bus. Of course, all governments are inherently bad, however, a Consciousness Coalition is necessary to establish cohesiveness, synergy, and direction. The U.S.O.B. congress allows our people to speak to the outside world with one voice. Moreover, for the Aquarian Age to truly dawn, consciousness must transition itself from an underground movement to a popular phenomenon.'

"Here is a list of our senators," Marlin went on, handing Melanie the sheaf of paper. "Collectively, they represent several million voting taxpayers. And our members are expanding daily. Heh, heh, heh. . . . . ."

Melanie looked down at the list of people in her hand. It read:

# USOB SENATORS

Senator from Rock Radio
Senator from Environmentalism
Senator from MTV
Senator from Electric Guitars
Senator from Natural Foods
Senator from UFO's
Senator from Mad Scientists
Senator from Natural Energy Sources
Senator from Alternative Newspapers
Senator from Life Extension
Senator from Recording Studios
Senator from Avant Garde Artisans
Senator from Underground Stores
Senator from Underground Nite Clubs
Senator from Rock Concerts
Senator from Static Electricity
Senator from Crafts Fairs
Senator from Wholistic Health
Senator from With-It Bookstores
Senator from Health Foods Restaurants
Senator from Fitness Centers
Senator from Wildlife
Secretary of Altered States

*Wow,* she thought, *this is the Government of The Future!*

"The United States Of Being," Melanie breathed. "I get it."

Melanie's eyes turned back to Marlin. This guy was not the type she was normally attracted to, but there was something about him that was......primitive. Maybe it was the beard. Suddenly the room felt warm.

"What do *you* do?" she asked him, tossing her hair back nonchalantly.

"I'm a video producer," he replied evenly. "Right now, we're producing an infomercial for screening in Congress. It's about the U.S.O.B.'s latest crusade— something concerning space. Would you like to see it?"

"Space always interests me," replied Melanie.

Maybe the viewing room would be cooler.

"Great," said Marlin. He got up from the desk and led her down a narrow hallway into a dimly-lit edit bay. A dozen small TV monitors mounted on a large instrument panel glowed out at them. Marlin slid easily into a padded chair and started punching buttons. Melanie sat down next to him and watched his hands moving smoothly over the controls. Above their heads on one of the monitors, a program began rewinding. A high squeal filled the air as the images raced backwards. Melanie noticed that it didn't feel any cooler in here and she was beginning to perspire.

*The machines,* she thought. *They must give off heat.*

Suddenly the squabbling noise stopped and the monitors froze. "You'll like this," Marlin said. He punched a button and the program began to roll. A title popped up. It said: "U.S.O.B. CRUSADE: SATELLITE AESTHETICS." Then the screen cut to four aliens standing on the bridge of an odd-looking spacecraft. They were peering out the windows. A conversation began among them.

"Hey, Irving. Let's check this one out. The blue one. With the white clouds. Pull into orbit."

"Right, Jack! What's Mrs. Preske's heap so far?"
"Look — It's got land masses! Doc—life form readings?"
"Affirmative, Captain. Humanoid lifeforms prevalent on all major land masses."
"Well, boys, whadda 'ya say we drop in for a closer look at this thing?
Dottie, prepare to energize transporter." Beeeooink!
"Hold it, Captain! Look — what's that?!?"

Outside the window, a satellite floated by. But not a usual one. This one had no body contouring or designer panels. Archaic solar cells supported by spindly aluminum appendages were flapping awkwardly in the solar wind. Worse, it had exposed nuts and bolts, silly saucer disks aimed at the ground, and chintzey krinkly aluminum foil. A real space eyesore.

"Jack, don't they ever clean up around here? HoooBoy, look at that," the Captain said.

"Larry! Hand me a copy of the *Encyclopedia of Cosmic Debris*, will you?
Thanks.
Yeah, here it is on page 240. Type 1A
Wow, that's like, raw junk.
We don't have to visit this place — it's a dive.
Let's go somewhere else more interesting.
Leopold! Ready? Hit it!"
"And Zoom —— Quark! They're outta here
and off to greener pastures," came an announcer's voice
out of the background.

Now the scene cut to a living room set where an actor
walked in and stood next to a crackling fireplace. He
spoke matter-of-factly:
"Meanwhile, below, UFO devotees are joining hands
around the planet, praying for a visitation.
Little do they know, they almost got one,
if it weren't for that cheezy tinker toy junk
floating around the planet.
No self-respecting world would ever launch trash
like that into its orbital space.
Are you kidding? It looks like something you get
in a cereal box.

"No wonder we don't have any Space Brother visitors
landing on the United Nations plaza!
They pull into orbit and see that low-tech
debris floating around the planet,
and they get, like, grossed-out
and spaaa-lit!

"If you people *wanna* have some Space Visitors,
then for gosh sake,
let's launch some halfway decent-looking satellites.
Make 'em out of paper mache if you have to,
but by all means, get 'em the hell up there.
Like pronto, Tonto!
And your motto can be:

---

**"Launch a Goodlooking Paper Mache Satellite to the Space Brothers For Christ and the Baby Whales Today!"**

---

Slowly the realization crept up on Melanie. It was *logical* for the USOB to be campaigning to clean up space so we could have extraterrestrial visitors. We *wanted* extraterrestrial visitors so they could introduce us to higher *states of being*. Which the *United States of Being* stood for. It made sense. It was right. And in that sublime instant of insight, something inside Melanie's mind went "...Ppffing!...." Suddenly a great feeling of release rushed through her, as if her mind were a large, overinflated birthday party balloon that Marlin let go from between his fingers, flying across the room. Pppffflllttggggkkk!

A music sting came up on the sound track behind the motto frozen on the video monitor. Marlin looked over at Melanie, a cocky grin on his face. "Pretty effective, wouldn't you say?"

Melanie didn't know *what* to say. Nova had been a beautiful, illuminating experience, but suddenly all of *this* was getting to be too much. She felt like she wanted to run out of the room, but then, something was holding her. She felt warm, very warm. She glanced down at her tan blouse and noticed it was wet underneath both of her arms. Quite wet, in fact. She started to feel embarrassed about the stains, but it turned into a giddy feeling. She felt lightheaded. Was it something the aliens had said? Sitting cross legged was so silly. She felt her breathing become shallow. There. Yes. There it is. Marlin's hand on her thigh. Finally. Good. That's better. Marlin. She needed Marlin. The video. Marlin's arms around her.

Yes. Marlin's lips meeting hers. Was there a video? Aliens? Ah, it's finally cooler. Clothes off. What video? Ah, that's what she needed. Marlin. Marlin had brought her back into this comfortable, dark room. This wonderful, dreamy, exciting room. She wondered if they ever made videos here.

# 23. KOLINAR CLEARANCE

Paula and Bruce hefted their sleeping pads into the wall compartments in the group's quarters. The eight friends had just returned from breakfast a few minutes ago. Behind them, Tara poked her head through the doorway into the chamber. Everybody turned around to greet her.

Tara held her hand up. "Good news," she announced. "You have all been granted Kolinar Clearance!"
A cheer went up in the room.
"Meet me in the Mindsurfing Area in fifteen minutes," she told them. "You will receive your pre-flight briefing."

Fifteen minutes later, the hotshot mindsurfers were assembled and ready. Alamar and Diana walked into the front of the room and smiled as everyone applauded.

"Congratulations!" Alamar began. "You've made it to the launching pad." As the applause subsided, he continued. "When you receive the fabulous Kolinar Clearance, you will be instructed to proceed through the confidential materials in a specific manner. This morning, we will give you a preview of what you can expect to encounter as you take off.

"First of all, the Kolinar Clearance is comprised of 67 **konads**.[1] The konads are newly-discovered hyperawareness triggers. They transform awareness into

---

[1] Rhymes with "gonads"

208

hyperawareness. Each konad is a springboard into a specific activity that you will perform. It will tell you to direct your consciousness down a certain avenue of action or perception. Over 25 years of research has gone into the discovery of the 67 konads. They are arranged very deliberately in a certain sequence to produce the **maximum** results. Heh, heh, heh......

"Secondly, you and your Navigator will do some warm-up exercises when you begin. Then your Navigator will take you through the konads as a team. He or she will train you how to perform the konads as you do each of them for the first time."

"Thirdly," Diana said, "after you and your Navigator have completed the konads as a team, you will then go back and do them again on your own."

"Assuming you still have hand-eye coordination, which by that point, you may not have," Alamar snickered.

"You will spend between thirty to sixty seconds on each konad," Diana continued. "Do not be in a hurry to do them any faster. A leisurely pace through the konads allows them to register more deeply. Don't be in a rush to get to the end. Don't be overcome by curiosity. Give your full attention to each konad. Go slow. Concentrate. Be happy. Enjoy yourself. Sit up straight. Tie your shoes. Eat your dinner. Put on a different shirt. Don't give me that look."

Bruce and Clark glanced at each other. "….Women...…" Clark grumbled.

Diana went on, "If you experience any astonishing effects or great realizations, stop the konad momentarily and go with the experience. You may wish to record your thoughts. When you have gotten all there is to get from the experience, begin the next konad.

"At some point, you will experience a sudden marked increase in your awareness. As you learned on the Mindsurfing Course, this is called a *Nova*. Sometimes Novas are accompanied by a new realization about life, and sometimes they are not. The main thing is that you will feel a gradual or rapid eruption of consciousness with an unmistakable intensifying of awareness. Some lucky people attain Nova quickly while they are still on the Mindsurfing Course." Everyone looked at Melanie. She smiled and blushed a little. "But when you graduate and do the Kolinar Clearance, you will all experience Nova on your way to Kolinar."

"There are several steps you should take when you get a Nova," Alamar said. Then he walked over to a white board in front of the room and wrote:

```
                    NOVA MANAGEMENT
A.      STOP DOING THE KONAD.
B.      RIDE THE NOVA. ( MINDSURFING )
C.      CLOSE YOUR EYES AND CONCENTRATE ON
        AWARENESS AND LIGHT.
        OR, KEEP YOUR EYES OPEN AND CONCENTRATE ON
        THE AIR AND THE SPACE IN THE ROOM. DON'T THINK.
D.      IF YOUR MIND WANTS SOMETHING TO DO, GIVE IT
        YOUR ROCKSTAR TO SAY.
        STAY OUT OF THOUGHTS. DO # C.
E.      RIDE THE WAVE UNTIL YOU GET THOUGHTS, THEN PULL
        OUT, AND GO ON TO THE NEXT KONAD.
```

"Don't sit there and think on step E," Alamar said. "That's a waste of time. Go right back to the materials and catch another wave." He made a vigorous paddling motion. Laughter rippled around the room.

"Novas can last anywhere from ten seconds to five minutes or more," Alamar continued. "Always manage a Nova using the procedures I've put on the board. You will get the best results this way."

Karin asked, "When will we get the Kolinar Clearance?"

Diana answered, "You won't. The Kolinar Clearance is issued only to professionally-trained and certified Navigators, who administer it according to rigorous standards of excellence. The Kolinar Clearance cannot be issued directly to individual mindsurfers, because the

211

materials are so explosive that some people would be overwhelmed. Therefore, Navigators are mandatory for every korbit. We will provide each of you with a Navigator tomorrow."

Alamar added, "Some people think the Kolinar Clearance contains secret information which, when you read it, will cause you to instantly attain Kolinar. This is not accurate.

"The konads are hyperawareness activators. If you perform them vigorously and to the best of your ability, under the right circumstances and with adequate preparation and supervision, you will attain Kolinar. But merely *reading* the instructions will not do anything. You have to know what to do, and how to do it, and then **DO** it!

"All of us are unique people, who will each experience Kolinar in our own ways," said Diana. The experience you are about to have may strike you as w a c k o , unless you're already half crazy. If so, don't worry!" She smiled. "We'll take you the rest of the way."

Alamar lowered the lights. "The confidential pre-flight clearance film you are about to see will answer any remaining questions you may have," he concluded.

\* \* \*

The film opened up with Rocco and an anchorwoman sitting in a living room stage set arranged with sofas, potted palms, and windows behind them. On the wall was a large picture of Mars.

"As I understand it," the anchorwoman opened, "this film is to be shown to Mindsurfing graduates who have been cleared for takeoff."

"That's right, Andrea," Roc replied. He faced the camera. "*You* who are watching this film have now entered the *KOLINAR CLEARANCE AREA*," he stated.

Goosebumps appeared on Kevin's forearms.

Andrea resumed, "I understand that you and I will be imparting confidential information to the students which is never to be discussed outside of this room. Is this the same data you shared with my class?"

"Yes," Roc replied. "So let's get to it," he gestured, shifting forward on the couch. "By the way," he mentioned to the audience, "Andrea's a Kolinar." She smiled.

"First, let's cover the practical application of what you've learned so far," Roc began. "The Zvortyl philosophy you have learned here can help you to broaden your outlook on life. Some of your values and priorities may be arbitrary, or even simply the result of social conditioning. Zvortyl can help you expand your personal horizons to new dimensions.

"Take table manners, for instance. In Japan, where my friend Maggie lives, it is considered to be a compliment to the chef if you belch. The louder the better.

"Lord knows we're buying enough Japanese products," Roc continued. "If their products are so good, why not their customs, too? So when it comes to the dinner table, what the hell. I say it's time to let 'er rrrrip!
In the spirit of cultural interchange, of course.

"Now on my home planet, Zorbitron, it is customary to insult your host as much as possible. See how customs are different everywhere? Now, *you* can apply this little gem of interstellar insight in your life right now."

"Okay," said Andrea, breaking in. "Let's take a specific example. Let's say you and your soul-mate are having dinner over at a friend's house. You are sitting a the dinner table, talking and enjoying a nice Italian r Out of the corner of your eye, you notice your n loading up a fork precariously full of cheese n ni. As the fork travels through space from plate to ome of the rebel macaronis start a mutiny and jump

"Now everyone's noticing as the almost-c ty fork reaches your lover's lips. And the thought is flashing through everybody's mind: 'Escaped macaroni! Leaving their cheesy trails all over the new carpet! Good thing we scotch-guarded that carpet! Just in case we ever had *slobs* over for dinner.' How would you handle that?"

"Good question," Roc replied. "Zvortyl in hand, you rise to the occasion and save the day with:

*'Don't worry, honey. The insects will get 'em.'*

"This gets your partner off the hot seat, insults your hosts, and demonstrates your knowledge of Nature all in one fell swoop. Moreover, it casts insects, one of God's booboos, in a heroic role, showing your generosity and reverberation with cosmic law."

Andrea smiled. "That's amazing," she said. "It really does work."

"See how easy it is?" Roc said.
"Philosophy has to be made
more *relevant* like this.
It has to address the *real issues*.
That's what this Party is all about."

"Can you give us another example?" Andrea asked.
"Sure," said Roc. "Take underwear, for example.
How can Zvortyl be applied here?

"Well, if your lover is frisky and playful
they probably have on funderwear.
Conversely, if they have a gas problem
they could be wearing thunderwear.
If they rrrrip one in public
it's blunderwear.

"If they can crack a joke that makes you laugh anyway
they must be wearing wonderwear.

Hey! Look at that big guy over there." He pointed to a heavy stage hand.

The camera followed. "He's wearing tonderwear."

"See the foxy blonde in tight jeans?" He pointed at the director. She smiled.

"She's wearing bunderwear. Or nonederwear."

Laughter off stage.

He looked out the window behind the set.

"That jogger across the street? Runderwear.

Myself? Punderwear.

"There.

Now wasn't that easy?

Do you see how Zvortyl can be applied now to real life situations?"

Andrea grinned. "Good," Roc said. "You win a cookie. And you may advance to the next level."

"Before they advance to that next level," Andrea said warmly, "did you want to cover the sighting in Bolivia?"

"Yes, of course," Roc answered.

The camera moved in closer on Andrea. Her voice shifted from a conversational tone into factual reporting. She began, "Forest Station D is a small log cabin on a three story high platform overlooking 150 miles of timberland in Bolivia. Last summer, a canister was recovered from the station containing a segment of film. The scenes you are about to see are highly confidential, and must never be discussed outside of this room." She signaled to a technician offstage. "On the monitor."

The clip came on. Rusty, Roc, and Alamar were sitting in the forest station, looking out over the green carpet of trees beneath them, drinking beer. They were having an animated philosophical conversation about something.

"So what's the worst thing that could happen?" Rusty asked his companions.

"Getting a pimple on prom night!" exclaimed Roc.

"No, even worse than that," insisted Rusty.

"Humankind bites the big one," burped Alamar. "We wipe out the chlorophyll."

"Let me set your mind at ease about that," Roc said, throwing his empty beer can on the pile.

"Earth life goes away.

And the answer is: So what?

There are a thousand planetary schools.

One of them fizzles.

Oh, well.

Stupid kids."

"What happens?" Alamar broke in. "I'll tell you. A few billion soul survivors take a number and stand in line to pick up bodies on different planets. And guess what. They pick up where they left off here."

"That's not the worst of it," added Rusty. "Somebody in Silver City Central notices a blip goes out on a screen. And they yell:

'Hey, Dwight! Look at this! Those stupid humanoids on planet Earth just wiped themselves out! Son of a gun. Dipshits.'"

Alamar grabbed a beer can and barked into it like it was a mike: "Hey, Ralph! It's Dwight. Yeah. Listen, get Johnny and the Dodge Boys to take a silver saucer over to Deneb Minor. Right. And tell 'em to start fucking the Neanderthals over there to start up a replacement school for Earth. Yeah, Earth. The dipshits just fried themselves. Okay? Roger."

Suddenly the scene changed from the timberland cabin to the bridge of a very high-tech spacecraft. Three crewmen sat at a console gleaming with electronic controls. Each crewman wore a name patch on their space suit. They were grumbling about something.

Tad:     "Oh, man, look at this, Biff. We gotta fly over
         to Deneb Minor. And look what we just pulled.
          Neanderthal Fucking Duty. Again."
Biff:    "What-a-drag. I hope these cavewomen are
         better than the last ones." He paused.
         "Remember the little one that bit Binky?"
Binky: "And the tall one in the treetop that teased Tad?"
Tad:     "Yeah, but do you remember the big buff babe
         Biff boffed?"

The film suddenly ended, evidently the last footage in the canister.

The living room stage with Roc and Andrea came back on. Andrea spoke first:
"Biff, Tad and Binky.
Preppies on patrol.
Space patrol.
Pulling Neanderthal Fucking Duty.
And all because
some big corporations on Earth
stir-fried the vegetation."
"Jeeez," Roc said.

The camera pulled back to a wide angle shot of Andrea.
"But it's just another day in the life of the Preppie Patrol, right, Roc?" she said.
"Right, Andrea," he replied. She continued:

"So listen, kids—
Don't worry about it.
In the Eyes of the Universe, it's all okay.
Let's make a buck on this blue green planet,
and no big deal if it goes away."

Roc and Andrea smiled at the camera, and white letters flashed on the bottom of the screen:

> The preceding was a paid political announcement by the
> Shoes for Industry Subcommittee.

After a few seconds, the white letters dissolved and the camera zeroed in on Roc as he got up and walked forward.

"Now you have all the training, all the preparation, all the essential information to make it," he said earnestly.
"Many have gone before you, and many more will follow you." He paused and smiled.
"My Navigators will get all of you through."
The camera moved in closer. Now all you could see were his crystal blue eyes.
"Good luck," he said. "I'll see you on the other side."

The screen went white.
And so did Brad's knuckles.

\* \* \*

Alamar gradually raised the lights in the room to a twilight level. The group slowly came back to reality. After a minute, Diana asked, "Does anyone have any questions about what you've just seen?" The party animals stared back blankly into space. Finally Bruce piped up.
"Yeah, I do," he ventured.
"What's that?" Diana asked.
"How do I get into space patrol?" he quipped.
Laughter rippled around the room.
Diana just smiled. "Buffer Day One begins tomorrow," she said, and adjourned the briefing.

# 24. WESLEYAN TUNNEL

Clark finished konad 67.
He had blown it out on konad 42.
But 67 was a major kicker.
He felt totally light.
His body felt like it weighed three ounces.
He had never seen the world like this before.
He rose in slow motion.

His Navigator placed a wide, royal blue ribbon over his head and it fell around his neck. Then the Navigator led Clark out of the room to where the others were waiting.

Within minutes, Alamar entered the chamber and addressed the graduates.
"Congratulations to each of you," he said with a smile.
"You were a motley crew when you first arrived," he told them, "but you surprised us all. Well done."
A warm feeling filled the room, adding to the intensity of the moment.

"Now that your eyes are open," Alamar continued, "you are ready for the Wesleyan Tunnel." Someone opened a doorway to the left. "Your experience tonight should be particularly interesting," he added with a sly grin.

Clark recognized Tara standing in the doorway leading to the tunnel. He had never seen her look so radiant. She signaled, and her students followed her through the opening and down a narrow passageway.

After walking a few hundred yards, Clark noticed the rock walls around him were giving way to white cinder blocks. The rock floor beneath his feet was also turning into smooth white cement. Then the passageway widened, and the group halted behind Tara in front of a thick glass divider.

"You are about to enter the Wesleyan Tunnel," she told them. Clark watched Tara's face, as her own experience of the tunnel came back to her with a smile. In a raspy voice she added, ". . . Pardy Hardy . . . "
Then she disappeared through a side door.

The eight friends slowly approached the entrance to the tunnel. As Brad peered through the glass, the tunnel looked like an ordinary underground service walkway running beneath a complex of buildings. To the right of the glass wall was a large rectangular gold plate. Etched into the shiny plate was the map of an island, with a single star on its south shore marked "BAYSHORE." Underneath this, near the bottom of the gold square, was a green jade button about an inch in diameter. After standing in front of it for a minute, Brad reached over and mashed the button. Nothing happened. Then slowly, a recorded voice emerged from speakers hidden in the chamber's ceiling. The voice spoke:

"Night is the Alternate World of starry skies by still waters where you can feel yourself exist and face the question of What Is Reality as it stares back at you.

"The differences between Earth and other planets are blatant in bright sunlight and subtle in cool moonlight.
"In the nighttime, things blend into one another, space is shortened, and time evaporates.

"Night cities from the air . . . .
could be cities anywhere.
Differences between objects, like expensive and inexpensive cars, become much less pronounced at night. They become cars in the night.

"Things are as if underwater, unified by the blanket of balmy breeze in the warm darkness. It's easy to find places that are not crowded or noisy at night. There's room to expand in, and you can own all you survey.

"The first thing that comes out in the morning is the newspaper, while the first thing that comes out in the night is the moon.

"At night there is unity with the other life in the galaxy. It is easier to lose time and location at night. You could be anywhere, anytime. You could even be on another planet. So you discover you are nowhere, and now you have truly arrived.

"You are standing on a moonlit beach; sea ahead of you, and to your right, a harbor with boats sleeping. The harbor scene is paper thin, like a still-life portrait. In front of you, the sparkling ocean flows over the faint horizon out into the glittering black sky. A gentle breeze warms the air to your touch, and night's blanket enfolds sea, stars, harbor and you.

"You have arrived at Nowhere, your final destination, and you have reached the point where philosophy actually begins."

The voice stopped. "Who was that?" asked Clark.
"I didn't recognize him," Amy answered, "but I think we're in the twilight zone."
The glass panel slid open.
The graduates slowly entered the passageway.

Ordinary hundred watt light bulbs set in the white cement ceiling illuminated their way. A feeling of anticipation filled the damp, musty air as the explorers moved down the corridor.

They started to notice cryptic messages lettered on the walls, along with small pictures painted in a rainbow of colors. Then they came upon a huge drawing of a bearded king standing on top of a giant muffin, his cape

# YES!  I want to join the party!

Name: _____

Address: _____

_____

Shoe Size: _____ Phone: _____

I want my Zvortyl Name to be: _____

*Please enroll me as a member so I can:*

- Enjoy the thrill and prestige of ***HyperAwareness***.
- Meet other wayward party animals and make new friends.
- Help put Rock'n'Roll in the driver's seat on The Moon and Mars.

| *Please send me:* |
|---|

____ Party memberships     @ $10 each    $_____

____ Copies of the book     @ $13 each    $_____

____ I want to make a donation.       $_____

I enclose:    $_____

Detach and mail to:
K O L I N A R    P.O. Box 937  Boca Raton, Florida  33429
*Make checks payable to KOLINAR.*     Florida residents add tax.

## Special Requests:

- ❑ Put me in touch with the nearest Zvortyl Party.
- ❑ Send me more info on Mindsurfing.
- ❑ Send me a catalog of Zvortyl party toys and stuff.
- ❑ Put me in touch with the Tubular Sorority.
- ❑ Send me more info on the United States of Being.
- ❑ Have the spaceship pick me up promptly at eleven.

### Please send info to my friends:

Name: _____

Address: _____

_____

_____

Name: _____

Address: _____

_____

billowing in the wind. An inscription was lettered to the left side of the drawing. It read:

> What is the infinite wealth?
> Behold!
> I am King Zanzibar of the ruffled muffet! A ruffled muffet is a muffet with ruffles in it. A ruffled muffet is a muffet that looks ruffley. . . .
> (Wow, this is really incredible to be talking like this.) King Zanzibar has his little golden palace on the top of the ruffled muffet. King Zanzibar has a beard and wears a blue cape. Yeah, and in his palace is a big jewel chest. An inside are a lot of blue purpose red orange yellow greane and purple jums. Jums are big jems. And the jems are a fair example of the infinite wealth.

Clark, Bruce, Karin and Paula exchanged dubious glances.

They moved down the corridor.

Fifty feet later, Amy discovered a six foot high light bulb drawn on the left wall, with yellow rays emanating around it some twenty feet in all directions. Above the bulb was the question again:

"What is the infinite wealth?"

Inside the bulb was lettered:

A thousand watt light coming from inside your body and piercing into the space in the room around you, illuminating the space in the room brilliantly. Only the light isn't light energy streaming into the space. Rather, it is pure awareness. Pure you. Or impure you. Whatever you can relate to. It ain't photons. It's yer *mind*, or whatever's left of it after you meet King Zanzibar.

Clark thought there wasn't much left of his mind before he entered the tunnel, and there were probably only a few stray molecules left of it now.

The eight friends pressed on down the tunnel, not knowing what to expect next. A few paces later, they came upon a gigantic star mural drawn on the right wall, spanning some hundred feet in length. At the far end of the mural, there was a recipe inscribed on the wall.

Earth

Milky Way
Politics

Rhombus
Region

Tarragon
Republic

Betelguese
Federation

Old
Galactic
Empire

Lomboid
Territory

Vedgulen
Armada

Zumptie
Rebellion

# Recipe For:
## Milky Way Potatoes

1. Take 40 <u>full</u> pounds of Chef Anton's
   toasted fried glibs, cubed and reheated to
   water before you're ready.
2. Bake for 30 civilizations. Attaboy!
   Now chow down and fasten your seat belt.
   Vaa Vaaa VOOM!!!
3. Paraguay over to the Tarragon Republic
   (spice mining), famous for its chicken.
   (See star map.)
4. Serve Milky Way Potatoes with your
   celebrity friends.
   Yum Yum Yummy in your tummy.
5. Wake up as a:  (choose one)
   a) waistoid waitron* on Betelgense
   b) demi-god of flying insects on Sex
      Planet No. 9
   c) cheese delivery specialist somewhere
      in the Zumptie Rebellion

   * Actually, you may be a waiter, a waitress, or
   an equal opportunity waitron.

*Milky Way Politics . . .*
*The secrets of our galaxy,* Karin breathed silently.
*This is priceless wisdom . . .*
*I think.*

*The star map!* Brad thought. *That's the key! The key to everything!*

*Cheese delivery specialist?* thought Paula. *What is this? Wisconsin?*

As they continued walking, the walls of the tunnel suddenly turned black;  probably painted that way by whatever protein-based life form had made the star map. The explorers pressed on.  After a few paces, the blackness began to give way to little twinkling stars, painted on the wall in sparkle glitter, that reflected the light from the ceiling.  As the friends advanced down the corridor, the population of sparkle glitter stars on both sides of the wall, ceiling, and floor grew more and more numerous, until they were gradually enveloped in a sea of stars.

Suddenly the stars around them gave way to gray rock walls.  Ahead of her in the distance, Paula saw giant handwriting on the left wall.  The markings on the wall almost seemed alive with energy.  The group came closer, slowly.  She could make it out now.  It said:

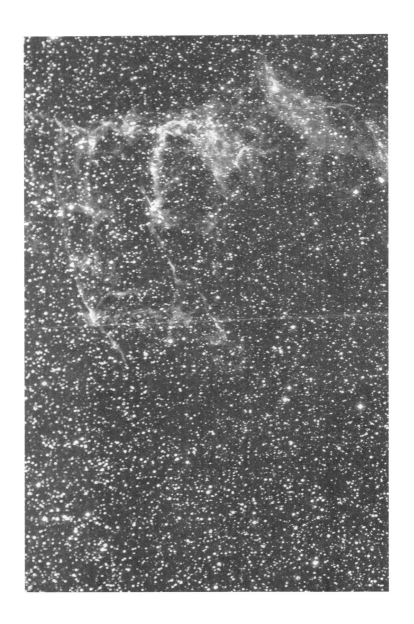

230

My Body Is The
Universe !
There Are Galaxies
Inside Me !
God I Feel
Beautiful ! ! ! ! !

I inhale galaxies.
I exhale galaxies.
God, It's
Beautiful !!
The Luminescance
of life throughout
the universe is
sparkelling .

232

Glittering
Radiant
Joyous
Awareness
!

OH !

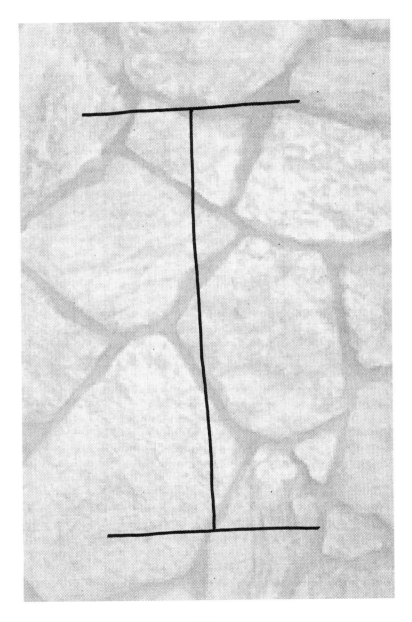

234

235

Hint: I made it out by
touring my apartment.
I have every light on.
I can see all of it at
once.   The bedroom. The
living room. Dining room.
Kitchen. Outside.
Galaxies.
Now I'm going to
keep on writing

without using the body's eyes. Yeah. I can see this writing and my body's eyes are closed. I can see light places the easiest like the kitchen but I do know where to cross my T's here!

238

239

I'm trying to bend over the corner of the door, move the door, and levitate the coaster. I ain't that good. Yet. But watch out world — Here I come!

What's unique
about me?
I'm free!
I can get
Out, Out, Out,
Out, OUT

Well, time for
another
gulp of
universe.

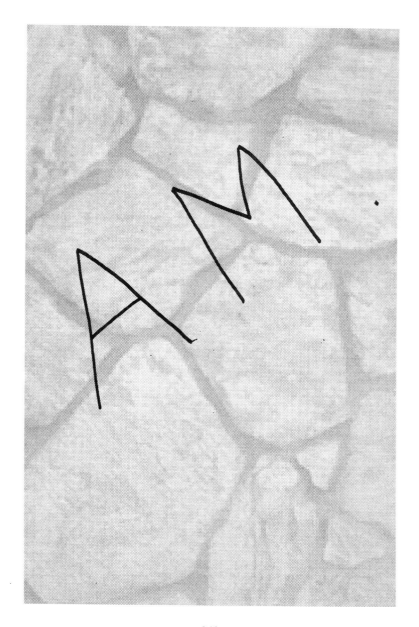

Nova is light.
Awareness is light.
Consciousness is the
light of the
universe. When
I close my
eyes, its

LIGHT
*in here.*
I AM
LIGHT

That's Kolinar.
When you all/
be the light.
In Mindsurfing,
concentrate on
LIGHT.

I have 10-20% of what I had at Bayshore.

I AM

I am sitting
here in
orgasm.
I am gasping
with Joy.

The Pleasures of Light!

This is not a
thousand orgasms
happening at once
like I had at
Bayshore. This is
like ten orgasms
happening at
once.

Laughing
Breathing
Coming
Gasping
Laughing

That's all
there is to
it, folks.

Joy!

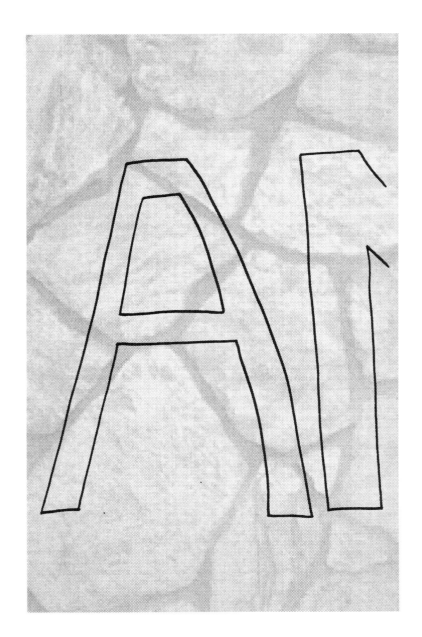

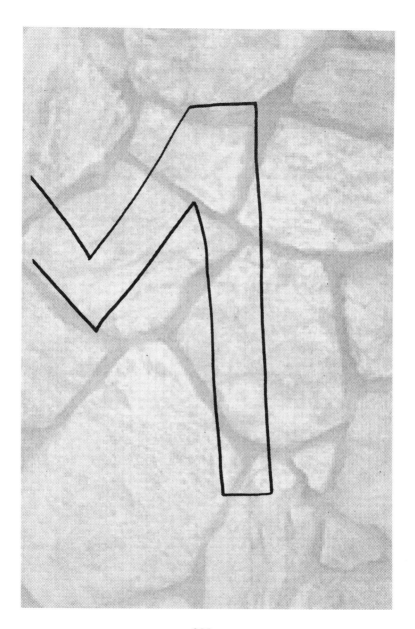

Here, let me try to burn it into the page for you!

257

Get the message?

# 25. <u>WRAP-UP</u>

The tunnel ended abruptly and emptied out into a huge, dimly-lit cavern filled with people. Rusty and Diana stepped forward out of the crowd.

"Congratulations!" Rusty roared. "You have just completed your quick-study course in (con)temporary insanity! You are now a certified looney-tune!"
Diana giggled, "Don't eat the bushes with the prickers on them, and you'll be fine."
"Was this a mindfuck, or what?" Rusty howled. "Hah?!?"

Clark found himself smiling. He looked around him. His friends were giggling. Karin made a face. Melanie thumbed her nose. Clark started laughing.

Paula looked around her and took in the scene. Globe lights in the faraway upper reaches of the cavern cast a dusky amber light onto the thronged interior, hinting at the great size of this rock-enclosed space. Paula estimated there were more than three thousand people gathered in the hall.
And more were coming.
The air was murmurous with people.

Rusty and Diana motioned for the group to follow them. Paula trailed Bruce as they wove single file through knots of people and up onto a rock embankment. From here, she saw a stage set up with instruments on a stone ledge in front of the enormous cave. Paula watched as two stage hands finished putting cymbals on a set of drums. She looked out at the multitude. There were at least five thousand people on the rock floor now.

And still they came.

Out in the desert, she knew, it already was red nightfall, but here in the cavern hall was perpetual twilight, a gray vastness thronged with men and women.

Paula glanced at her companions, sharing the moment, and waited as the hall filled. After a few minutes, a spotlight from somewhere in the roof of the cave suddenly hit the empty stage. She felt the hush come over the crowd, some seven thousand people now, standing silently almost without movement.

A man walked out onto the stage and over to a microphone. A roar welled up from the floor. Novak smiled, and received the greeting.

Then he held up his hand.

"Before we start," he said, "I have a confession to make." The cheering gradually subsided. Novak explained:

"Now this may be a shocker, fellow rockers,
but I have been to —ahem— The Symphony a few times.
I did it as an occasional favor
when I was dating the cute classical music teacher, Peg Shapely.
In other words, rockers,
I had ulterior motives,
so it was cool.

"Actually, though, there were a couple of times it wasn't
too bad.
The symphony would set up in a meadow near a country
inn at dusk.
The audience would sit around it
on a grassy hillside dotted with willow trees.
When I arrived with my date,
we'd bring a picnic basket
of ample size,
then spread our checkered blanket
on a grassy rise.
We'd listen to the music
under starry skies,
and nobody would notice
my hand between her
. . . . . er . . . . .
Pies! That's it. Blueberry and apple.
What's a picnic without a pie, right?
Right.
No, just kidding, folks, really."
*Yeah, sure*, thought Paula.
"Anyway, the symphony was
not what you would call *good* music
by any stretch of the imagination,
but, I did have to admit
that it was well-*orchestrated* anyway.


"There are, like, 76 people playing different instruments
together, like violins, cellos, French horns and oboes.
And with that many different pieces, you can get some

—mildly—interesting blendings of sound. And occasionally, when everyone is playing full blast, you can get something that sounds pretty triumphant.

"Not that I am in *favor* of it or anything. In fact, symphonies should be taxed. Those stiffs in tuxedos need government bullshit more than *we* do. Let *them* pay for it."
The crowd responded.
"But anyway, a full symphony orchestra at its heroic crescendo is like a itty bitty mouse going 'squeak, squeak, squeak' compared to a *new* kind of sound that *you* know something about, you low-lifes."
The hall reverberated with shouts and whistles.

"Let me ask you——What IS it that could enable *half* a dozen long-haired guys playing instruments to TOTALLY OVERPOWER 76 people? Six versus 76, and 76 gets flattened like a steamroller truckin' over a wayward pop-tart.

"What could it be?!? Magic? Faith in Miracles? Higher Education? What?
What could do that?"
The crowd exploded.

"What's that you say?"
"Huh?"
"Rock something?"
"Like a rock?"
"Oh. Rock'n'Roll?"

"Is that it?"
"Oh, really?"

Huge, magnificent, earth-shattering but melodically beautiful power chords crashed through the cavern as Rocco's three guitarists strode in unison down parallel isles through the throng. The crowd tipped over the edge. When the three reached the stage, the rest of the band was ready, and the place took off like a tornado.

Paula went with it. The sound was circling around the room like a cyclone. Several seconds of music were alive all at once. It was like in an echo chamber. She couldn't understand it. Then it hit her. *The walls*, she thought. *They're solid rock. It's perfect acoustics.*

For the next hour, Paula lost herself in a primitive frenzy of joy, merging with the crowd and the music. When it was over, the band left the stage in a fiery blaze of thunder echoing in the hall.

Pitch black dark swooped
down over the feisty crowd.
Like some Great Voice of Rock'n'Roll,
hoots, hollers, stomps and whistles
rose up out of the cheering throng.
*These people are ALIVE!* thought Paula.
*They're **bristling** with energy! They're obnoxious!*

And all of a sudden, what looked like
hundreds of candles started to appear
in the deafening darkness.
*No——Look*, Paula realized, *it's not hundreds.*
*It's THOUSANDS of candles, burning in the night,*
*at every level, high and low, all around the*
*huge cavernous pitch black hall.*

A spotlight hit the stage and Novak was back at the
microphone. His words echoed in the grotto:
"*This* is the Wave of the Future, my friends.
Every candle is a lighted mind.
Each soul powered by Rock'n'Roll,
steering their way to the stars.

"Come with us, then, into the night.
The Gateway of Heaven opens on high.
Liftoff erupts with a thundering might
and our Rock Concert hurtles up into the sky.

"But waitaminnit," he said, stopping abruptly.
"You know there's a message behind Rock'n'Roll.
You know it has meaning for you and the other people at
the concert.
You know we all share a common set of values,
and with Kolinar in our hands, there's no stopping us.

"But get real, man. We may be singing our songs, and
having our concerts, but don't kid yourself.
The Preppies are in control.
They're the ones who are running America, not us.

"And even though we're right,
and we're playing our music as loud as we can,
they just smile and close the mansion windows,
and smugly pass control of this country
on from generation to generation.

"The 'Mighty' Preps—the Big Money—are only *one
percent* of our population, but they control a THIRD of
this nation's wealth.......
The 'Total Preps'—the whole Old Boy Network—are
*five percent* of the population, but they control over HALF
of our nation's wealth.

"Where does that leave **you**, Pardy Hound?
Out howlin' at the Moon?"
The people howled back.
"We have the truth, but not the power.
And remember, Big Money got no soul."
The crowd hooted.

"The Preps don't want you to be conscious. They want
you to buy more floor wax for that lasting shine.
Buy buy buy buy buy.
More more more more more. Screw consciousness."
He paused.
"So what are we gonna do about it?" he asked them.
They cheered him. He smiled, and went on.
"Well, history has shown that it's a lot easier to form
*n e w* societies than it is to reform old ones.

So, we have to be like the Pilgrims......

"You see, four hundred years ago,
the Pilgrims didn't hang around and try to
change England.
That would have been a waste of time.
They said: 'Fuck England. We're leaving.'
And so can you.
So, we don't have to change America.
We have to *LEAVE* America."
The crowd roared.

"What the hell do you think is gonna happen in 2040 and
2080 and 2150?
We're gonna split!
We're gonna take to the stars and get the hell *outta* here!
And we're gonna do things *our* way on the Moon and
Mars.

"This is *your* future, buddy.
*You're* going to reincarnate into this bullshit whether you
like it or not.
Save yourself.
Take action *now* to point the course of events in the right
direction for *you*.

"And what *is* the right direction for your future lives?" he
asked the crowd.
"MARS!" they replied in a single voice.
"Leave the Preppies behind!" Novak yelled.
" MARS IS OURS ! "

The cavern went apeshit.

"The Zvortyl Party will bring fast lane korbit to you and
your wayward friends," he continued.
"But we will do more than that.
We will also set in motion the forces that will put
Rock'n'Roll in the driver's seat
on the Moon and Mars.

"The Preps will colonize Mars to open new markets for
their floor wax.
That's a given.
But what they aren't counting on is a Martian
underground.
And that's where we come in.

"It looks like there's a lot of time,
but we have a big job ahead of us.
We are starting now.
We are building a new community.
And when the time comes, we will be ready....

"We will change the face of the desert planet.
We will make rivers run in the red rock forest.
And we will SHAKE the Martian sky with Rock and Roll!

Roll !

Roll !

Roll !

Roll !"

# YES!  I want to join the party!

Name: _____

Address: _____

_____

Shoe Size: _____  Phone: _____

I want my Zvortyl Name to be: _____

*Please enroll me as a member so I can:*

- Enjoy the thrill and prestige of ***HyperAwareness***.
- Meet other wayward party animals and make new friends.
- Help put Rock'n'Roll in the driver's seat on the Moon and Mars.

| *Please send me:* |
|---|

_____  Party memberships      @ $10 each    $_____

_____  More copies of the book  @ $13 each    $_____

_____  I want to make a donation.            $_____

I enclose:   $_____

Detach and mail to:
K O L I N A R   P.O. Box 937 Boca Raton, Florida  33429
*Make checks payable to KOLINAR.*          Florida residents add tax.

i

## Special Requests:

- ☐ Put me in touch with the nearest Zvortyl Party.
- ☐ Send me more info on Mindsurfing.
- ☐ Send me a catalog of Zvortyl party toys and stuff.
- ☐ Put me in touch with the Tubular Sorority.
- ☐ Send me more info on the United States of Being.
- ☐ Have the spaceship pick me up promptly at eleven.

## Please send info to my friends:

Name: _____

Address: _____

_____

Name: _____

Address: _____

_____

# YES! I want to join the party!

Name: _____

Address: _____

_____

Shoe Size: _____ Phone: _____

I want my Zvortyl Name to be: _____

*Please enroll me as a member so I can:*

♦ Enjoy the thrill and prestige of *HyperAwareness*.
♦ Meet other wayward party animals and make new friends.
♦ Help put Rock'n'Roll in the driver's seat on the Moon and Mars.

| *Please send me:* |
|---|

_____ Party memberships      @ $10 each    $_____

_____ More copies of the book @ $13 each    $_____

_____ I want to make a donation.            $_____

I enclose:    $_____

Detach and mail to:

K O L I N A R   P.O. Box 937 Boca Raton, Florida  33429

*Make checks payable to KOLINAR.*        Florida residents add tax.

iii

## Special Requests:

- ❑ Put me in touch with the nearest Zvortyl Party.
- ❑ Send me more info on Mindsurfing.
- ❑ Send me a catalog of Zvortyl party toys and stuff.
- ❑ Put me in touch with the Tubular Sorority.
- ❑ Send me more info on the United States of Being.
- ❑ Have the spaceship pick me up promptly at eleven.

## Please send info to my friends:

Name: _____

Address: _____

_____

Name: _____

Address: _____

_____

# OTHER BOOKS BY THE SAME AUTHOR

## A History of French Cheerleading

Traces the development of pom-pom girl cheerleading in France from medieval jousting tournaments to modern day rugby.


## 101 Mothball Ornaments You Can Make (For Christmas)

Add an aromatic flair to your Holiday decorating with these festive, unusual ornaments. Includes step by step instructions with diagrams.


## Self-Realization Through Transformational Fingerpainting

Mr. Rockit reveals the little-known secrets of using this powerful primary art form to unlock your Inner Mind's hidden potential. Comes with handsome seminar notebook.


## Suntan U. - A Guide To Southern Colleges

Get smart and a great tan too at these swingin' Southern schools. Contains listings of 117 universities in all, complete with major party locations.


## The Book of Bowling Trophies

Fully illustrated in color, this high-quality hardbound edition will be a proud addition to your family library.